Contents

The Authors

John Inglis won a trade union scholarship to Ruskin College Oxford to study Economics, was awarded a travelling scholarship to Australia and New Zealand, and subsequently read the Historical Tripos at Trinity College Cambridge. Since 1966 he has taught in further education and is now a senior lecturer at Barmulloch College in Glasgow. He is a part-time tutor-counsellor and admissions adviser in the Open University, is deeply interested in the problmes of mature students, and runs study skills courses for Open University students in Scotland.

John Inglis is married, has three children and enjoys camping, hill walking and fishing in the scottish countryside.

Roger Lewis

Roger Lewis has taught in primary and secondary schools, and in colleges of education. He has been an Open University tutor since 1971. For a while he worked as a Staff Tutor for the Open University, and he has taught adults at evening class and for the National Extension College. For NEC he has written *How to Write Essays, Wordpower* and *Studying Poetry,* and co-authored *The Arts: A Fresh Approach* and *Use Your Dictionary!* In 1967 he joined the drama department of Leeds Polytechnic, and in 1980 he started work for NEC in the tutorial and counselling area. He is married with one son.

1. Proposition and argument

1.1. Introduction

Arguments have a habit of going wrong. They sometimes end in ill feeling, with people throwing abuse at one another. Or they may ramble on for hours, wandering from one topic to another until at the end of the argument it is still not clear whether any progress has been made, or whether anyone has changed his mind. Often these difficulties could be avoided if the people concerned thought more clearly and organised their arguments better.

Some arguments of course, are not easy to settle one way or the other. There are no simple 'right' answers or solutions to questions like 'Is Capitalism better than Socialism?' or 'Should the dealth penalty be restored?' or 'Is there a God?' These are questions that fascinate people, and challenge them to sort out complex arguments. Each of us must make up his own mind. It is, though, important to decide what we think and to explain the reasons for holding this view. It is also important to listen to the opposite case and to get clear the arguments offered by our opponents. Usually we only half-listen to the other side, and this means that we are not able to answer their arguments as fully as we might, or maybe even to change our own mind.

Those of us studying courses which involve the writing of essays also have difficulty in organising our thoughts clearly on paper. Chief examiners are always complaining that candidates do not 'stick to the point', do not 'answer the question set'. It seems hard for many people to discipline themselves to this; it's too easy (whether talking or writing) to follow red herrings and to end up in confusion.

To help you to overcome these problems we set out a *method* in this course. If you persevere with this then you will be better able to argue clearly and relevantly yourself, to assess the arguments offered by other people and also to look at both the structure and the content of arguments.

It is no good just listening to advice; you must practise the method, and so we provide many exercises for you to work through. If you carry out the procedure suggested then you will be able to apply yourself immediately to the problem. You will work systematically and devote more of your attention to the ideas you are working with, whether they are your own or whether you are working on someone else's written word. Our method can be reduced to a few basic principles which can be committed to memory and will become a tool of study that you can use in any situation requiring consideration of your own or of someone else's ideas.

The development of our method springs from a conviction that every person who sets out to write something, or to make a speech or even to paint a picture, has something that he wants to prove and if we systematically examine what they say, we can understand what their intention was — and whether or not they succeeded in realising it. People are often not clear themselves about what they want to say, but if we can learn to detect this quickly we have an advantage because we will have spotted the weakness of their argument and so we will be able to argue about it more effectively. Let's now look at this question of intention in an actual example.

SAQ 1

Read the following speech and then answer the questions we put after it. You will probably need to read the speech through two or three times. Keep your answers to all these Self-Assessment Questions together, in a book or file.

Ladies and Gentlemen,

It gives me great pleasure to say a few words of appreciation for Harold Smith on this occasion of his retirement dinner.

Harold, over the many long years he has spent at this College, has endeared himself to everyone with his tact, his unfailing good humour and his steadfastness. My first memory of Harry is still quite clear. It was on the very day that the college opened and he had the job of getting rid of a stray dog which had wandered into the Assembly Hall during the official opening and I may say he managed that task with a smile on his face.

In those early days the college was really a very small and rather homely place, and most of you here would not recognise it. There was no swimming pool then and we used to take the college bus down to the local baths. The workshops were all in the main building then and this very hall we are sitting in used to be the gymnasium. The teachers' staff room was so small that we had to stagger the tea and lunch breaks and even then we were practically sitting on each other's lap.

Yes these were balmy days all right with small classes and quite low teaching loads — the average then, I think was about eighteen hours a week and visits by the Inspectors were quite regular and everyone took them very seriously indeed.

And we had some characters here in those days. There was old Sam Brevitt who had such a sonorous voice that he used to put his students to sleep and it was not unusual for us to hear snores coming from his room and when you looked in the whole class, including the teacher, was asleep. Some of you will remember Mr. Trail who was a self-appointed expert in Spiritualism and he used to take the craft boys for English and his favourite lesson was to conduct a séance. You could pass his room and find it in complete darkness with the class sitting round a table, hands outstretched, invoking the spirits to enter.

Yes they were happy days and now they have gone and so too has Harry. Let's all raise our glasses and wish him every happiness and a long and eventful retirement.

Answer the following questions – briefly:-

1 What did the speaker set out to do in his speech?

2 What was his speech, in the main, all about?

3 Did the speaker do what he set out to do? If the answer is 'no' then what went wrong?

4 Look at your answers and connect them up into a brief paragraph about the speech.

When we stop to ask you questions like this, always stop to answer them, and write down your answer in a study notebook. Don't read our *Discussion* until you have made your own attempt, as that is the best way to learn. Then compare what you have written with our ideas.

Discussion _____

Have you answered the questions yourself? If not, do that before reading on.

How did you get on? I suppose it is not always good to be too critical of others because the speaker was plainly a kindly person who liked to reminisce and who also liked the person, Harold, who was retiring.

The speaker, however, did not really carry his intention out fully. He set out to say some words of appreciation for Harold but most of his speech was about the college, its early days and some of the worthies who had once worked there. All that he had to say about Harry could have been put in one long sentence, and he really should have said more about the man himself. The opening of his speech shows that he is aware of what it is he should be doing, but he wanders from the point. He is sidetracked, and becomes irrelevant until he suddenly returns to the point at the very end of his speech. These faults of irrelevance and poor organisation are very common ones.

1.2. Definitions

We shall be using certain words time and time again in this course. In this section we shall set out our definitions; from here on this is how we shall be using these words.

Proposition: a statement of what a speaker or writer wishes to prove (e.g. he may want to convince his audience that there should be fewer cars on the roads).

Argument: unfortunately, for the purpose of this course 'argument' has two meanings:-
1) the overall case made by a speaker or writer (including the

proposition)

2) the individual reason or justification for saying that the proposition is true. The important difference between this and the former sense of 'argument' is that here we refer to the *separate* points made in justification of the proposition; sense 1 refers to the case as a whole.

THE OVERALL
ARGUMENT
'WE SHOULD RIDE
BIKES'
SENSE 1

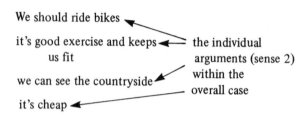

SAQ2

To test your understanding of these two uses of the word 'argument', please answer the following question.

Look at the two definitions of the word 'argument' given above. Say which definition ((1) or (2)) is being used in each of the statements that follow.

1 His argument was that capital punishment should be brought back.
2 The third argument in his case was faulty.
3 He put forward a very clear argument for joining the club.
4 Some of his arguments for joining the scouts were very strong.

Discussion

1 Used in sense (1) – his overall argument (or case) was for the restoration of the death penalty.
2 Sense (2): one of the arguments within a case.
3 Probably sense (1), though this could also be sense (2).
4 Sense (2) – the individual arguments.

There's at least one other meaning of 'argument' – the exchange of views between two or more people (e.g. 'They were having a noisy argument'). But this use is not important for us now.

SAQ3

Let's now turn to another example of an actual argument. The following passage is part of a report on training in the clothing industry. It was written by a manager trying to convince his colleagues that more training is needed. As before, read the excerpt two or three times, and answer the questions printed beneath it. Then compare your answers with our discussion.

It is my firm conviction that we need more training in the Clothing Industry because the machines they are introducing are becoming more and more complicated.

Consider, for example, the PFAFF range of machines. There are now more than 100 basic models and specific-purpose machines. Some of these are high speed machines and they come with lock-stitch, chain-stitch, single and double needle machines. Some have different feed machanisms and there is also a bewildering variety of hooks and shuttles.

Mechanised sewing units are now spearheading technological development and these are improving productivity and profits. These units can do everything that the industry requires. They can sew long seams, do dart closing, and make button holes and all at high speed and in mass production. There are also machines which will cater for extra fullness in sleeves and armholes of sackcoats, overcoats and similar garments.

The latest development from PFAFF is the use of mechanised sewing units and integrated sewing stations which set the trend in industrial sewing and no modern factory can afford to be without them. Our industry should be grateful to this company for their exciting range of machines which is helping to make our job easier and our industry more profitable.

1 What did the man set out to do; i.e. what was his proposition?
2 How many arguments (using the word in the second sense) can you find in this passage?
3 How many of these arguments are relevant to the writer's proposition?
4 Given his aim, can you suggest anything else which could have gone into his speech?

Connect your answers to these questions into a brief paragraph.

Discussion

1 His proposition is that more training is needed in the clothing industry because of the increased sophistication of the machinery now in use.
2 He uses three arguments. The first argument is that the Pfaff machines are highly sophisticated and of great variety. The second is that mechanised sewing units are revolutionising the industry's output and profit, while the third is that the use of integrated sewing stations is setting new trends.
3 In fact, the only really relevant part of his report is the first sentence. His arguments are intended to support this, but he fails to make any further reference to training, either as it now exists or as it could be managed in the future.
4 He does give good evidence to support his contention that the machinery is

becoming increasingly sophisticated and we might say that he is implying that this means that more training is necessary. Implying something, though, is to leave too much to chance: the writer hasn't justified his case.

This passage shows another common weakness, very often found in student essays. Much of the material could *be made* relevant, but isn't quite. It's too easy to leave the reader to complete what should have been the writer's job, and that is to locate, explicitly, the relevance of the material to the question asked.

1.3 Proposition and Argument
Now we have looked at some common weaknesses in written and spoken arguments. The first step to remedying these is to be able to distinguish the proposition of the overall argument (Sense 1 of 'argument') from the individual arguments supporting it (Sense 2). You have already been practising identifying the proposition (what the writer/speaker is trying to prove) in the earlier Self Assessment Questions. In the following example (a letter to a newspaper) we take this a little further. Read the extract two or three times before you read on, but this time there are no questions for you to answer.

Sir,

The reintroduction of capital punishment would be a retrogressive step and I ask all those who call for it to consider the following arguments.

There is firstly no evidence to support the argument that capital punishment acts as a deterrent or that the existence of capital punishment would make murderers think twice. Most murders are committed in the heat of the moment with no time to think about the consequence.

It cannot be denied also that mistakes can be made and when this happens innocent people have to go to a violent death. In such a case the State is setting the citizen the worst possible example. We hear a lot about violence these days – violence in the cinema and on the television and it would really be unforgivable were the State to indulge in violence, because violence usually begets violence.

Those who advocate capital punishment frequently overlook the fact that the true purpose of punishment in our judicial system is the reform of the offender and it goes without saying that you cannot reform a dead man. If we all were allowed to indulge our desire for revenge then our society would become a most unpleasant place to live in.

Yours faithfully

First check through for relevance. Does the writer keep to the point? We think he does.

We want to look at the way this passage is organised – its *structure*. We are not concerned here with whether or not we agree with the content of the passage, but only with whether the passage is well argued. It is worth remembering that we can have an untrue proposition that is supported by good and relevant arguments or a true proposition that is supported badly. Here we are looking at the structure rather than at the truth of the arguments.

Remember these definitions of proposition and argument as we shall be using them frequently from now on. Perhaps you should write the definitions down in your notebook or file, and then check back to Section 2 and make sure that you are clear about them.

Here is our analysis of the structure of the argument. It seems to us to be well constructed and the writer does stay relevant throughout, unlike the examples given earlier. (There are slight problems about the argument but we'll be returning to these later.)

Capital Punishment

Proposition   The writer is trying to prove that it would be a backward step for this country to reintroduce capital punishment and that if we do the country will become a less pleasant place to live in.

Arguments

1 The first argument states that capital punishment is not a deterrent since most murders are committed in the heat of the moment.

2 Mistakes have been made and innocent people have been hanged.

3 Violence is a major problem these days and the State should not set a bad example by doing violent things.

4 The aim of punishment is to reform criminals and you cannot do this if the criminal is dead.

5 Lastly, if the motive for capital punishment is revenge then this might encourage us all to indulge our own desires for revenge and our country would become an unpleasant place.

We hope that some of the advantages of trying to separate proposition and arguments will have become clear to you. For one thing you can summarise the whole argument on a single page and this enables you to check arguments against the proposition to find out if they are relevant or not. If you did temporarily forget what the proposition was you could quickly look back and refresh your memory.

There are other advantages too. You can quickly compare the arguments with one another and find out if any are simply a repeat of earlier arguments. If so, you can quickly discount it as a new argument and say 'You have already made that point'.

Once you know what the proposition is you can quickly check to see if the same mistake that we saw in the earlier passage has been made, i.e. where the person strayed from his main purpose and did not manage to do what he initially set out to do.

Now for some practice in identifying propositions and arguments (used in the second sense, again!)

SAQ 4

Read the following passage and underline the sentence which includes the proposition.

> Those who talk glibly of getting tough with social security 'scroungers' ignore the fact that most people prefer to work for their living. It is true that in the days of full employment there was always a pool of unemployed persons but this tended to be made up of married women just leaving work, of seasonal workers temporarily employed and a few unemployables. However, as long as there were jobs on offer the majority of people preferred to work so that during the 1960s and for a part of the seventies, the numbers out of work were less than 2% of the work force.

Discussion

You should have underlined the first sentence. If you haven't, check back and see whether the sentence you underlined states the main idea as clearly.

SAQ 5

Read the following three passages several times. When you have decided what the proposition is in each case, write it down in one sentence. Use your own words if you can.

1 It is a refreshing thing to witness the widespread introduction of continuous assessment testing as a means of examination in our schools and colleges. The formal type of examination where the candidates were closeted for three hours often favoured those who had good memories or a special facility for expressing themselves; but it often did not elicit who could think, and people could also be lucky in finding topics which they had happened to revise. Another point is that formal exams are easier for those who have a good nervous equipment and who stand up to strain and stress.

2 There should be no place in Britain or in British politics for political parties which preach race hatred and who encourage violence as a solution to political problems. Theories of this type were responsible for the holocaust of the 2nd World War and for the horrors of the concentration camp.

3 The low polls in local and national elections are a disgrace and a blot on our democratic way of life. Citizens have an obligation to take an interest in affairs; to listen to the policies of the various parties and to make up their

minds about them and to vote in accordance with their conscience. Voting should be made compulsory and a fine should be imposed on those who neglect this civic duty. This system works well in Australia where the ordinary man in the street has a high living standard.

Discussion

1 It is good to see the increasing use of continuous assessment in our schools and colleges.

2 Political parties which support racism and violence should not be allowed in Britain.

3 Low polls are a threat to democracy.

Read through the passages again and check that you can see that these are the points being proposed, and that the rest of the passages contain arguments to support these propositions.

SAQ 6

Read the following passage through several times and then answer the questions.

Mr. Chairman,

There is no doubt in my mind that democracy is a much better system of government and society than dictatorship.

In the first place democracy is a more open system of government and more people are encouraged to use their talents for their own and for the common good.

Some people think that we should leave our problems to be tackled by one powerful dictator, but society now is so complex that no one person can know all the answers to every problem.

The death of a dictator can often leave a power vacuum if no one has been fully briefed to succeed him, and periods of absolute dictatorship are often succeeded by spells of anarchy.

Finally, 'Power corrupts,' as the quotation goes, and 'absolute power corrupts absolutely'.

1 What is the proposition?

2 Briefly list the arguments.

Discussion

1 Democracy is a better system of government and society than dictatorship.

2 a) Democracy is more open and because of this individuals can use their talents.

b) No one dictator could solve the problems presented by a complex
   society.
c) Problems occur when a dictator dies.
d) A dictator tends to be corrupted by his power.

(Your answer may differ slightly from ours. But don't worry about slight differences.)

1.4   Interlude : Your own views
You will notice that we have been concentrating throughout on the structure of
arguments, and not on whether we *agree* with the ideas and opinions themselves.

SAQ 7 _____

Why are we not concerned about the actual content of the argument? e.g. about
whether *we* feel capital punishment should be brought back or whether democracy is better than dictatorship?

Write a sentence saying why you think we are ignoring our own views and
feelings.

Discussion _____

Because our concern is with the way the arguments are constructed, and with
what makes a soundly organised argument, we are trying to suggest to you the
characteristics of good arguments; you can then use the structure yourself.
(Sense 1 of 'argument'!)

This we feel is also a good discipline in itself. It's all too easy for us to weigh
in straightaway with our own views before we've taken the trouble to organise
them or to listen to those of our opponents.

WE CAN'T RELY ON OUR VIEWS BEING SELF-EVIDENT. THEY NEED TO
BE WELL SUPPORTED.

1.5   Composing your own argument
You have practised looking at the structure of the arguments of others. You
have identified propositions and listed the arguments used to support them. We
should now like you to construct an argument of your own because as we
pointed out the course has two main aims:

1 to help you to find your way around the arguments of others and to look at
   them critically
2 to help you to construct sound arguments of your own – in speaking and
   writing.

We now turn to the second of these aims.

SAQ 8

'Mothers ought to be at home and not at work'. Do you agree?
Decide which side you are going to argue on:

- mothers should be at home, or
- mothers should be at work, and

1 state your proposition (what you are trying to prove) in the first paragraph
2 write two or three arguments to prove your proposition, giving one paragraph to each argument.

Remember that it's the *structure* of your argument that we'll be looking closely
at.

Discussion

Here is one possible argument.

Mothers ought not to be at work
It is my belief that mothers ought not to be at work because motherhood
should be a big enough task for any woman.
A mother who comes home after a day at the office or in school will be tired
and irritable and she will not be able to give her children the love and attention which children must have if they are to become well balanced adults.
In these days of high unemployment mothers are often at work and their
children are on the dole. This is wrong and unfair.
Another problem when mothers are at work is that of the latch-key children.
Children are coming home from school and since mother is at work they get
into all kinds of mischief, stealing from supermarkets and so on.

In this example the proposition is clearly stated in the first paragraph. This
enables the reader to check to see if each argument is in fact relevant. The arguments are clear and related to the proposition. (It will not always be necessary to
keep one point to a paragraph, but it's a useful thing to do in the early stages,
and helps you to keep the argument clear.) The skill of keeping each point relevant to the proposition is an important one when writing essays, too.

Assignment A
The two parts of this assignment provide you with practice in some of the skills
taught in Unit 1. Send both parts to your tutor and he will help you to perfect
your understanding of the unit.

Part 1
Read the following passage carefully, several times. Then

1 write down the proposition (in your own words if possible)
2 briefly list the arguments the writer uses to prove his case

3 say whether you think the passage is well argued or not, and why.

Sir,

Why don't those people who are constantly knocking our industrial society start looking at some of the advantages that we have over those who lived 100 years ago.

Consider the great increase in life expectancy. Men can, in the main, expect to live until they are over 70 and women have an even greater life expectancy. Our doctors and scientists have eradicated some of the most painful diseases and are controlling many diseases which used to be fatal.

Look at the standards of comfort and convenience which we now have in our homes — our central heating, gas fires, dish washers, washing machines and vacuum cleaners. We are now so well served that many women, using these aids, can go to work and still keep a nice home and look after their children.

Think about our welfare and social services too. Our Welfare State is comprehensive and no matter what misfortunes may befall us there is a benefit for every emergency.

NB Keep a copy of your notes on (1) and (2); we will look at these again in Unit 2, possibly before your assignment is returned.

Part 2
Construct your own argument on one of the following. Do this by

1 deciding which side you are on, and stating this clearly in the first paragraph as your proposition
2 writing at least three brief arguments to support your proposition, using a new paragraph for each argument.

You may, if you wish, construct a *spoken* argument on a cassette. In this case you follow exactly the same procedures. Make sure that your recording is clear.

NB If you wish, you can try more than one of the questions.

a) 'We should get more for our rates.' Do you agree?
b) 'We should buy British goods.' Do you agree?
c) 'Violence and sex on TV should be banned.' Do you agree?
d) 'Adult education should be free.' Do you agree?
e) An argument of your own choice.

Send your answers to the two questions (1 and 2) to your tutor. You can also let him know of any difficulties you are meeting with the material so far.

2. Topic and point

2.1 Introduction

In Unit 1 we introduced two important terms

- proposition
- argument.

You will remember that 'argument' had two meanings.

SAQ 1 _____

Write a sentence on each of the meanings, as follows:

1 A proposition is . . . .
2 'Argument' in its first sense means . . . .
3 'Argument' in its second sense means . . . .

Discussion _____

1 A proposition is a statement of what a speaker or writer wishes to prove.
2 'Argument' in its first sense means the overall case a speaker or writer makes to prove his proposition to be true.
3 'Argument' in its second sense refers to *one individual* justification of the proposition.

In Unit 1 you practised distinguishing a proposition from the arguments used to support it, and you practised writing your own arguments.

But sometimes arguments are longer and more complex than those we looked at in Unit 1. This means that the structure of the overall argument is often more complicated, and that there are more opportunities for getting confused or lost (whether you are speaking or writing an argument, or listening to or reading it!)

With longer arguments it helps to refine further our simple distinction between proposition and argument and in this unit we will show you

- how to break individual arguments up for closer scrutiny
- an effective method of setting out the structure of an argument (Sense 1!) in outline.

But first to look at a common difficulty with some longer arguments: the split proposition.

2.2 The Split Proposition

SAQ 2 _____

Read the following passage through carefully two or three times and then answer the questions printed beneath it.

Microprocessors

The two major political parties frequently pose as antagonists but they are both misleading the public over the effect that these microprocessors will have on unemployment and on all our lives in the fairly immediate future.

Both parties will suggest that they are capable of reversing the present trend towards greater unemployment but there is not a lot of evidence that they were doing this before the silicon chip began to come on to the market. The present government has now given the microprocessor industry a capital grant and its official blessing.

Experts in the Common Market predict that because of the present rate of job wastage, unemployment in the EEC could be in the region of 20 million by the mid 1980s and a high percentage of these will be young people who will never have known the experience of work.

The social problems associated with unemployment will increase — there will be more vandalism, criminality, deviance and one can also expect an upsurge in extremist politics. We should never forget that the Nazis came to power in Germany at the height of the Great Depression.

This problem cannot be ignored because it will not go away. The fact is that it is going to call for a radical change in our attitudes.

1 What is the writer trying to prove?
2 What arguments does he use?
3 Do the arguments relate to the proposition?

Discussion

1 What is important here is that the proposition seems to be placed partly in the first and partly in the last paragraphs. This is a characteristic of some arguments, and you need to be alert to the possibility of the proposition being split like this. It doesn't really help either writer or reader, as we'll go on to show.

The author is trying to prove the following case:

Microprocessors will cause more unemployment (Paragraph 1) and affect all our lives (Paragraph 1). So we shall have to alter our attitudes radically in order to cope with the changes (last paragraph).

2 His arguments are mainly related to the first part of his proposition (i.e. as stated in Paragraph 1) and particularly to the likelihood of greater unemployment . He states

a) that the political parties have been unable to reverse the trend towards unemployment even before microprocessors came on to the market; it is unlikely that they will be able to do so now.

b) that Common Market experts predict high unemployment as a result of job wastage (If his facts are right, this seems a reasonable argument.)

c) that there will be an increase in social problems as unemployment increases.

3   These arguments seem to relate reasonably well to the first part of the proposition. But he says little about the second part of the proposition – i.e. that we shall have to alter our attitudes. We need to know more about this before we can be convinced!

Now if this writer had put his proposition all in the same place (the first paragraph) then he might have noticed this weakness and have given us some ideas about how we might prepare ourselves for a future Europe with 20 million unemployed.

Notice how our analysis has revealed a defect in the structure of the argument. We have seen how the writer has slipped in a major point without apparently being fully aware of what he has done. Learn from this when constructing arguments of your own. State the proposition fully at the start and go on to deal with the whole of it. Constantly check each argument against the proposition to make sure that you are on the right lines.

2.3   Topic and Point: Breaking each argument down

In Unit 1, we analysed the structure of whole arguments into proposition and the separate arguments used to support it. We now move on to a further subdivision of each argument into *topic* and *point*. This will enable us to prepare an outline plan of an argument and to see whether the argument as a whole is clear and consistent.

Generally speaking, each new paragraph introduces a new theme, a further argument.

SAQ3 ───

Look at the use of the word 'argument' in the above sentence. Is it being used in Sense (1) (the case as a whole) or Sense (2) (the individual links within the chain of the argument as a whole; the individual 'arguments')?

Discussion ─────────────────────────────────────

Sense (2). We are going to look at each individual argument, and to divide it into *topic* and *point*.

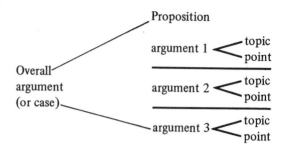

Each time we have a new argument, we have a new topic: some new theme is introduced, a new idea is given. This theme relates to the proposition. We call this new theme a *topic*.

The point is what is said about the topic. The distinction between topic and point will become clearer when we look at an example. Read the following passage through. (You came across it before, in Unit 1.)

1 The reintroduction of capital punishment would be a retrogressive step and I ask all those who call for it to consider the following arguments.

2 There is firstly no evidence to support the argument that capital punishment acts as a deterrent or that the existence of capital punishment would make murderers think twice. Most murders are committed in the heat of the moment with no time to think about the consequence.

3 It cannot be denied also that mistakes can be made and when this happens innocent people have to go to a violent death. In such a case the State is setting the citizen the worst possible example. We hear a lot about violence these days — violence in the cinema and on the television and it would really be unforgivable were the State to indulge in violence, because violence usually begets violence.

4 Those who advocate capital punishment frequently overlook the fact that the true purpose of punishment in our judicial system is the reform of the offender and it goes without saying that you cannot reform a dead man. If we all were allowed to indulge our desire for revenge then our society would become a most unpleasant place to live in.

Look back to Unit 1 pp. 8, 9. There we analysed this passage into proposition and arguments. We are now going to sub-divide each argument into its topic and point.

Capital Punishment

Proposition: The writer is trying to prove that it would be a backward step for this country to bring back capital punishment and that if we do the country will not be such a pleasant place in which to live. (Notice that the proposition is split between Paragraphs

1 and 4. This is one of the 'slight problems' about the argument that we mentioned in Unit 1.)

Topic	Point
● A deterrent? (Paragraph 2)	● No evidence for this – most murders are committed in the heat of the moment with no thought for consequences.
● Mistakes. (Paragraph 3)	● Can and have been made and innocent people die.
● Violence. (Paragraph 3)	● The State should not set a bad example – and add to the growing trend of violence.
● Purpose of punishment. (Paragraph 4)	● Is to reform – you can't reform the dead.
● Passion for revenge. (Paragraph 4)	● If we all did this the country would become a less pleasant place.

Now for you to practise dividing arguments into topic and point. In the assignment for Unit 1 you were asked to look at a passage on *Life 100 Years Ago*. You had to write down the proposition and to list the arguments used by the writer to prove his case. Look back over what you wrote.

SAQ 4

We want you now to take the analysis one stage further, by analysing each argument into its topic and point. Look back over this section to make sure that you understand what you have to do.

Discussion

Life 100 Years Ago

Proposition: Life today is much better than it was 100 years ago.

Topic	Point
● Life expectancy.	● Men and women live much longer.
● Diseases.	● Many have been eliminated by our doctors and scientists.
● Standards of living.	● Much more comfort about; women can earn more and keep a house.
● Welfare service.	● We are protected against all emergencies.

Your answer may be slightly different, but do you see how the *topic* is the new idea, and the *point* is what is said about that new idea? The topic is thus at a more general level than the point. The topic introduces the theme and the point goes on to say something more specific about it. Together they may add up to an argument that supports the proposition.

Compare your answer with ours. If yours is very different, and you can't see why, then ask your tutor for his advice.

SAQ5

For further practice before trying your assignment, look back to the passage on microprocessors. State the proposition of the passage, and then break down each argument into topic and point.

Discussion

Proposition: Microprocessors will adversely affect our lives and we must make radical changes to accommodate them.

Topic	*Point*
● Unemployment.	● Already a well established trend which major parties cannot stop.
● Silicon chip.	● Now that it is coming on the market it will add to unemployment (really topic 1).
● Common Market Experts	● Forecasting 20 million unemployed by the mid 1980's.
● Reports.	● (Point is that this is not only an expert study but it is independent of Britain.)
● Social Problems.	● Associated with unemployment – will increase – can cause extremism. Historical precedent for this is Nazi Germany.

This is a rather more complex example. Notice our comments in brackets: the method we suggest is not inflexible. You'll often need to comment in the way in which we have done here, to indicate any difficulties or further refinements in the arguments.

Assignment B

Part 1

Read the following passage carefully two or three times and then answer the following questions. Before you do this please quickly review the Self-Assessment Questions in this Unit. Please try not to get drawn into the content of the arguments; at this stage of the course we are trying to concern ourselves with structure, with the way the arguments are organised.

Strikes

The events of this and the most recent winters have surely brought home to government and people that we must as a nation find a solution to the strikes which have crippled our transport, parts of our industry, our hospitals and even, alas, our graveyards.

Strikes are enormously costly and really bring no benefit to anyone. The strikers lose several weeks' wages and then they invariably settle for more modest figures than those they went on strike for – e.g. local government workers. Strikes also cause shortages and this usually results in higher prices for everyone and once the new price has been attained the shopkeepers are reluctant to bring it back down again.

Our external balance of trade also suffers. The goods we export accumulate on the docks whilst our imports are held back too, and during all this time we are in doubt as to how much we owe and how much we have earned. This often results in financial uncertainty and can cause speculation on the pound. The dockers' strike of 1967 precipitated such a crisis that the government was forced to devalue the currency by 15%. A most unfortunate effect of this was that many poor countries overseas who held sterling at that time lost huge sums of money they could not afford to lose and we in Britain finished up paying more for the goods we imported.

One does not have to have any training in economics to know that time lost in production because of strikes can never be regained. The goods we could have produced are lost to us for ever and in a country where there is a lot of poverty, a lack of housing, and many social problems, this is disgraceful.

Employment also is affected by strikes because many small firms are not able to survive a period of say six weeks without getting any revenue in and if they have an overdraft they can find themselves in financial trouble. Also if the strike is successful and the wages bill has to rise by 20% then many small firms go out of business because they cannot make profits at that level of wages.

Trades unions must accept that things have changed since the war. They do not represent a downtrodden and servile working class any longer because no one really wants the old days back again. Unions today have the respect of government; they serve on all manner of government bodies and the recent government has passed a host of laws which give the unions protection in important things such as Health and Safety, Redundancy, Unfair Dismissal, Contracts of Employment.

The best way forward would be to have an arbitration system which would limit the right to strike in exchange for more legal protection. Disputes could be settled by skilled conciliators and law could replace the use of force. The money saved could be a tremendous financial boost to our ailing Health

Service. This system, I might add, works well in other countries notably in America, in Australia and N.Z. and all of these countries are known to have affluent working classes.

Questions
1 What is the proposition of the argument on strikes? Did you experience any problems in finding it? If so state briefly what these were.
2 List the arguments used to support the proposition.
3 Break each argument down into topic and point as in Self-Assessment Questions 4 and 5.
4 Assuming the arguments to be correct, do you believe the passage to be structurally sound? List any criticisms which you have (e.g. do the arguments relate to the proposition?).
5 Look again at your answers to the four questions and using these as a basis write a paragraph of about 100 words on the structure of the argument.
Send your answers to Questions 1, 2, 3, 4 and 5 to your tutor.

Part 2
You have now had plenty of practice in working on the distinctions between proposition, argument, topic and point. You have looked at the structure of the arguments of others by breaking them down analytically. Now try to construct your own arguments by preparing an outline plan.

Choose one of the following titles:-

1 'High rise flats have been a disaster.'
2 'Income tax is too high.'
3 'Religion does more harm than good.'

Choose one of the following two ways of working. (Read both ways first).

First way

● First of all state the proposition you wish to argue for, in one sentence (or two at most).

● Then prepare an outline of the topics and points of each of your arguments (just as you have been doing in this unit).

● Next write up your argument into continuous prose, using your outline as a guide.

(Send your work at all three stages to your tutor.)

Second way
Some students may want to write a rough draft of their answer before an outline just to get their thoughts moving. In this case the sequence would be as follows:

- Decide which side you're going to argue on.

*• Write your argument in continuous prose, but only in rough draft.

- Check that your proposition is clearly stated and that your arguments support it.

*• Then construct an outline, using the topic-point division.

*• Check that this is a sound outline and make any necessary modifications.

*• Then write up the answer from this outline.

(Send to your tutor your work at the stages marked *)

Whichever method you choose:

- state your proposition clearly

- ensure that each argument is related to the proposition

- make sure that the topic of each argument is clearly stated and expanded by the point.

Then send your work on parts 1 and 2 to your tutor as your assignment for Unit 2.

3. Assertions

3.1 Introduction

In this unit we shall conclude our look at the structure of arguments by outlining the differences between an argument and an assertion. But first, to revise the points made so far, answer the following Self-Assessment Question.

SAQ 1 _____

In your own words, write a definition of:

1 proposition
2 argument (2 senses!)
3 topic
4 point.

Discussion _____

1 Proposition: a statement of what it is a writer or speaker wishes to prove.
2 Argument (1): the overall case presented.
   Argument (2): the individual ideas or justifications given in support of the proposition.
3 Topic: a new theme or idea introduced as part of an argument.
4 Point: what is said about the topic.

3.2 The Assertion

Look at the following statements:

1 'The Scottish people definitely want self-government.'
2 'Leaders of Third World countries in the United Nations favour industrialisation because of the material and social benefits it confers.'
3 'War promotes cruelty, vice and stupidity.'
4 'War is a good influence in that it is necessary for the growth of strong states.'

We call these *assertions* because they are flat statements which would need further evidence before they could be accepted as arguments. An assertion is thus characterised by the two following characteristics.

1 It is a flat statement − 'this is so.'
2 No evidence is offered in support of the statement.

People often use assertions and think they are offering arguments. An argument goes beyond flat statement and offers evidence in the form of reasons or other kinds of justification.

SAQ2

Write down two or three common assertions – e.g. about coloured people, taxes, the unions, management, schools.

Discussion

There are many possible answers! Here are a few:-

1 'Teachers are too soft with children these days.'
2 'British management is inefficient.'
3 'Taxes are far too high.'

Check these statements, and those of your own, to see that they have the two characteristics of an assertion as mentioned above.

So assertions are often offered in place of arguments. For an assertion to become an argument, evidence has to be produced. Or, to use the terms we introduced in Unit 2, a topic and point are needed.

SAQ3

Read the following two statements. Which is an argument and which is an assertion? Give a reason for your answer.

1 'Industrial arbitration will not work in Britain.'
2 'All industrial disputes should go to an arbitration board. The system works well enough in other countries and indeed in many instances in this country.'

Discussion

1 is just an assertion. No argument is offered. The flat statement needs further support before it can be considered as an argument.
2 is an argument. It offers evidence: there are comparative examples which we can study, and we can also examine selected areas in Britain where arbitration works. Of course we should have to think about the argument before we could accept it, but at least it *is* an argument. It has a topic (the arbitration system) and a point ('it works in other countries and in places here too'). You'll notice that 2 is longer than 1. The trouble with assertions is that they are often short and sweeping (we say that they are 'sweeping statements'). As soon as we think more carefully about what we are wishing to prove then we tend to *qualify* what we say and offer supporting evidence. Thus we need more words.

3.3 Reasonable and unreasonable assertions

It is important to remember that some assertions may be reasonable. We take some things for granted and, depending on the context, don't need to provide evidence for some statements. For example:-

1 'Human life is precious'
2 'Roads should be safe for pedestrians'
3 'People derive comfort from their religion in times of trouble'

are assertions which scarcely need supporting evidence in Britain today; though it's possible to think of situations where they *would* need careful arguing, e.g. (for the first statement) when the country is at war.

Also, a lot can depend upon who makes the assertion. If, for example, the statement 'Industrial arbitration will not work in Britain' is made by an acknowledged expert in the field then it may be considered reasonable because his experience and knowledge can stand as a kind of unspoken evidence. The writer would not be able to include everything; he would draw upon his vast knowledge of the subject and at certain places he would make positive statements where he was absolutely sure of his facts and this would allow him to take us into the area of the subject he considered important.

At the same time we must be careful, because experts can be wrong and can use their expertise to support views or parties outside their specialist area. And not even experts should be exempt from providing good arguments in support of what they believe.

SAQ 4

Look back to the four assertions given at the start of this unit. Read each one carefully, and say whether you consider it reasonable or unreasonable. Give reasons for your decision in each case.

Discussion

1 'The Scottish people definitely want self-government.'

On its own this doesn't seem to us a reasonable assertion. How can we know that a whole nation wants something? We really do need evidence here, perhaps in the form of a well-tested and properly administered opinion poll or maybe in the of the results of a recent general election in which very large majorities were secured by S.N.P. candidates. It scarcely matters who made this assertion: no amount of authority or expertise can make it reasonable.

2 'Leaders of most Third World countries in the United Nations favour industrialisation because of the material and social benefits it confers.'

This is reasonable. It is, for a start, much more carefully phrased than (1). Note the use of the word 'most' — this allows the person making the statement to be challenged and admits the possibility of there being exceptions. Compare this with 'definitely' in (1). The assertion makes a generally accepted statement about development: poor countries try to acquire the expertise and aid of developed countries to increase their industrial base, as a way of breaking into a new phase of social and economic growth. We are talking about a small number of people (leaders of Third World countries) in the United Nations. It would be possible to examine their viewpoint in some detail. We also know that the UN seeks to promote industrialisation through trade and aid. Further it is a fact that the largest Third World countries (India and China) are actively pursuing industrialisation. The assertion is, in fact, well on the way to becoming an argument. Notice that it contains more words than (1) — remember that we said that this can often indicate greater care in making a point.

If this statement had been made by the Secretary General of the UN then it would be supported by his particular experience and knowledge. But the statement would probably be so generally agreed to that it wouldn't need extra support of this kind.

3 'War promotes cruelty and vice and stupidity.'

Most people in our society would consider this reasonable. Few would disagree with it and it wouldn't need any special authority to back it up (though eye-witness authorities could easily be found). Evidence of physical and mental cruelty can easily be seen on our television screens most nights. It is worth pointing out that what is a 'reasonable' assertion is largely a matter of opinion and extent of knowledge. We are inevitably influenced by what our society considers 'reasonable'. There are no clear hard and fast rules that we can apply. We must make our own minds up. There are, though, certain criteria we can remember, i.e. Who is making the assertion? Is the assertion likely to be acceptable today in our country? Is the assertion one that we as individuals could accept?

4 'War is a good influence in that it is necessary for the growth of strong states.'

Whereas the previous statement on war (3) would be generally agreed, this one is much more difficult. The point being made seems to depend upon political and historical factors. It could be argued (and has been) that in a situation where many small states on a continent are in constant conflict then the only way to achieve stability is for some states to become bigger at the expense of others, by conquest, and eventually to embrace all the others in a unified state. This was probably true of Italy in the Sixteenth Century. On the other hand, to achieve stability in this way must inevitably involve much short-term suffering, and there are other ways of achieving stability than war, e.g. through organisations like the United Nations, or through federation.

So this statement needs much careful development and further discussion. We're not at all sure whether to put it in the reasonable or unreasonable category. As with many of the other examples we really need to see the context in which the assertion is made before we can judge fairly.

SAQ 5

Now read the assertions that follow. Take each one and

1 say whether you think it is reasonable or unreasonable

2 say *why* you think it is reasonable or unreasonable.

(NB We think that there are probably two reasonable and two unreasonable statements.)

1 'Knowledge can be pursued and is worth pursuing.'

2 'The Fall of the Roman Empire had far-reaching consequences for the history of mankind.'
(Aurelio Bernardi, an Italian Professor of History, wrote this in an essay which subsequently became part of a book on the economic problems of the Roman Empire, edited by Carlo M. Cipolla.)

3 'Large-scale unemployment is more of a blessing than a curse.'

4 'Marriage as an institution is finished.'

Discussion

1 This comes into the same category as (3) in Self-Assessment Question 4. Most people in our society would agree with this, so it is a reasonable assertion. Notice, though, that it is so general a statement as to be almost meaningless (a common problem with assertions). Are *all* forms of knowledge worth pursuing, and can they all be pursued with equal ease? The assertion thus needs turning into a more substantial argument.

2 This is another reasonable assertion. We may know little about Roman history, but we will respect the experience and learning of the man who is making this statement, and we notice that it is taken from a scholarly work. It has further authority behind it in that the essay has subsequently been placed in a book on the economic problems of the Roman Empire, edited by another scholar.
So the experience and knowledge of the man making this statement makes it credible. He is, after all, speaking on his own subject.
Even so we should remember never to take statements on trust but always to seek further evidence. In the case of this statement, for example, we would look for a definition of the 'consequences' (what were they, exactly?) and for an attempt to prove that these consequences were the result of the fall of the Roman Empire and were not brought about by other causes.

3 We think that this is an unreasonable assertion considering the view our society (and the whole of the western world) takes of unemployment. The

UN and the EEC state in their charters that to work is a basic human right. All parties in Britain subscribe to the ideal of full employment (at least they do in theory) and most people would agree that unemployment is unpleasant. It is also generally agreed that unemployment helps to create social problems such as vandalism and violence. Thus to make an assertion such as this would involve the author in a very great deal of argument and explanation of his reasons for believing it to be true. He could argue, for example, that while unemployment is an evil there are greater evils, such as those caused by inflation, and that unemployment may be needed to combat these. (Notice, though, the phrase 'large-scale'.)

4 We think that this is an unreasonable assertion. Maybe the writer is thinking of divorce rates, but even this evidence (if he had given it) would be questionable since presumably a proportion of divorces lead to further marriages, and most couples still seem to choose to marry.

Maybe the writer means something else, e.g. that marriage stifles the individuality of the people concerned. But this cannot easily be proved, and certainly cannot be taken on trust.

SAQ 6

Looking back on it now, we can see, in spite of many obscurities in our defective records that the invention of printing, as we commonly call it, was more than a signal that enormous changes were to come. (From *Early Modern Europe (from about 1450 to 1720),* by Sir George Clark, Regius Professor of Modern History at Cambridge.)

Would you accept this as a reasonable assertion? Give two reasons.

Discussion

Sir George Clark is a scholar of high reputation and he is giving his expert opinion about the impact of printing over a sustained period. Not only is he an expert but he has framed his assertion in quite a cautious manner indicating that if we ever made up the obscurities in our defective records he would still not be too far wrong. Thirdly, it is fairly well known that printing did have an impact on society and it could easily (from the layman's view) be seen how this could come about. Sir George Clark is not relying on authority alone.

3.4 Points to remember

You will notice from the discussions of Self-Assessment Questions 4 and 5 that there are not always clear-cut answers to the questions we ask. It is very important to use our judgements, and to think in a flexible way about the nature of our arguments and about those offered to us by others. What we are mainly concerned with in this unit is to alert you to the dangers of using assertions and to the incompleteness of the assertion as a form of argument. You should now be able to identify an assertion and to challenge it if necessary.

We have been looking at the assertions of others so far in this unit, but the general points made apply also to your own speaking and writing. You should be aware by now of the need to

- state your points carefully
- offer evidence for them
- use a clear structure.

Your work on assertions in this unit should lead you to ask questions like the following; for example when you are writing an essay.

- Have I made any assertions?
- Are they reasonable?
- Do I need to make them more substantial by adding extra evidence?
- What kind of evidence do I need?

But in our concluding Self-Assessment Question we want to look again at structure, for while a proposition supported by assertions may look quite good, it may be structurally weak.

SAQ 7 _____

Read the following passage and answer the questions at the end of it.

Sir,

Why is it that so many people take such delight in attacking the popular press? It seems that the more successful these papers are the more violent is the attack upon them. This often comes as a shock to those who enjoy their daily news and who also find, in the papers, a source of information and comfort.

The popular press is able to write about the complex problems of the day in down-to-earth language which the ordinary man can understand and so it performs a useful social function. A fine example of this was the lead up to the referendum on the Common Market when the popular press provided a platform for all the different views.

The ordinary people of the country are loyal to the popular press. They know the facts are printed without fear or favour.

The fact of the matter is that the critics are totally confused about what the popular press is trying to do; they cannot see that it is out to preserve the liberty of the individual.

Yours,

1   Prepare a brief outline of proposition and argument (This as you now know

involves breaking each argument down into a topic and point.

2 The writer intended to use three arguments at least but some of these are assertions. Select and discuss at least two assertions.

3 What evidence do you think is needed to strengthen the assertions?

4 Write a sentence or two summarising your answers to the first three questions, stating why this argument as a whole is weak.

Discussion

1 The following outline would be an acceptable one.

Proposition: The popular press does not deserve the attacks made upon it because it performs a useful social function.

Topic	Point
● Today's problems.	● The popular press reports them in language which the ordinary man understands.
● Loyalty.	● The readers are loyal.
● Facts.	● Fearlessly printed.
● Critics.	● Are confused about aims of the press – they don't see that the press is out to preserve liberty.

2,3 Argument (1) is quite reasonable. It is well known that the popular press sets out its ideas in a series of short paragraphs and that the language used is uncomplicated. We could also quickly check to see if this was the case. And, of course, if it does make issues more comprehensible then the press does provide a useful function. This argument supports the proposition.

Argument (2) is more of a problem. The fact that the readers are loyal may be evidence that the popular press does fulfil a useful function and should not be attacked but the statement that the readers 'are loyal' is simply an assertion which would need to be supported. One could look at circulation figures or at evidence which would indicate loyalty, e.g. if, after a period of the paper being out of circulation, it comes back to find that its circulation returns to the former numbers, we might regard that as evidence of loyalty. But for all we know people might buy the paper because of habit, and some would say that the press is not necessarily fulfilling a useful social function. The paper could be popular because of the quality of the racing tips or because it folds into the pocket and can be read in a crowded train.

Arguments (3) and (4) are also flat statements which seem to need further support; for example the writer could discuss instances of fearless reporting (for argument (3)) and extend his assertions — 'the critics are totally confused' and 'the popular press is. . . out to preserve the liberty of the individual'.

4 The argument is weak because it comprises a proposition supported by one
argument and two or three assertions. The assertions would have needed
further evidence and some of this would not have been easy to find.

Assignment C

Part 1

Read the following passage at least twice before answering the questions printed
after it.

Sir,

The inflationary pressures of the last few years have made it imperative that
we decide, once and for all, to introduce a national minimum wage.

The concept of a minimum standard of living is now well known in our
society. We now have family incomes supplement to make income up to what
is necessary for a family to exist at the barest level, and there is no disagreement about what constitutes low pay — any family man earning £45 a week
or less is low paid.

We are now on the threshold of what promises to be another technological
revolution as the computer and the micro-processor make more people redun-
dant. This will flood the labour market with the unemployed so that
employers will be able to pick and choose their employees and will also be
able to force wages down. The benefits of the innovations must be properly
shared out and a national minimum wage would be a fair way of doing that.

The low paid are often low paid because they work in unskilled or unproduc-
tive jobs. They work in occupations where trade unions are not strong. In
times of rapidly rising prices the low paid tend to get left behind while
skilled workers who are organised into effective unions, or who produce
articles which are in high demand, are often able to get rises to keep pace
with inflation.

A national minimum wage of, say, £60 a week for all over 21 would be a
declaration by the State that all those who work must receive a decent
remuneration for so doing. This wage would then be linked to an index figure
and it could thereafter be adjusted to keep pace with rises in the cost of
living.

One objection to the idea of a national minimum wage is that the skilled
unions would resist it on the ground that this would erode the differentials.
This is not so; the trade unionists of this country are solidly behind the idea.

Others from the business world would argue that a minimum national wage
of £60 a week would result in increased unemployment but we all know that
this is a spurious argument.

A minimum national wage would ensure that the average family man with
a wife and two children would have enough to support his family in a decent
standard of comfort and it might even encourage more wives to give up work-

ing and return to looking after the home and family. This would make more jobs available and families more stable.

Yours etc...

Questions:-

1 What is the writer trying to prove? (i.e. State the proposition.) Use your own words as far as you can.

2 List the arguments, detailing topic and point.

3 Are there any assertions?
   a) State which you regard as reasonable and which are unreasonable.
   b) Give reasons for your decisions, and state what further evidence the writer could usefully provide to give support to his opinion.

4 Write a brief paragraph on the structure of the passage, stating why you believe it to be sound or weak. (Your outline (1) and (2) above should help you to do this, and a checklist has been included as Appendix 1. You should consult the checklist when answering this part of the assignment.)

Part 2
Collect at least four examples of assertions from any source — e.g. friends, colleagues, family, newspapers. Certain radio and television programmes are often good sources of assertions — e.g. *Any Questions, Any Answers,* people being interviewed on news programmes. Try to include at least one example of each kind of assertion, and give your reasons for deciding whether each is reasonable or unreasonable.

Appendix 1: Checklist for a soundly constructed argument

1 The proposition is clearly stated and easily identified.

2 The arguments relate to the proposition and do try to prove it.

3 The arguments are presented in an orderly fashion.

Bear these points in mind when analysing the structure of any argument you are presented with. They will help you to look at the framework of the case offered.

4. Suspect types of argument:1

4.1 Introduction

So far in this course we have been emphasising the *structure* of arguments. When we isolate arguments from the proposition we are attempting to lay bare a chain of reasoning, particularly in the written or printed work we encounter. We try to reveal the extent to which the arguments support the proposition and also the way in which the arguments relate to each other. We have also looked at the structure of the arguments themselves (their topics and points) and have seen the dangers of unreasonable assertions.

In this unit, and the next, we shall look at the arguments themselves and concentrate on the effectiveness of each individual argument. Your work on structure will now be complemented by practice in looking at different types of argument.

4.2 Types of argument

We want you to become aware of the types of argument frequently used and which are, in various ways, suspect. Once you can identify these you can be on your guard against them. In this unit and in Unit 5 we shall look at the following:

1 persuader words
2 emotive language
3 generalisations
4 analogies
5 familiar appeals
6 conflation
7 rhetorical questions
8 syllogisms

4.3 'Persuader' words

Sometimes certain words are used with the intention of persuading you to accept particular opinions as 'obvious'. If you're not careful, you càn be carried along by this device and you then fail to look at the quality of the argument offered. Beware of words like:

- obviously
- plainly
- clearly
- surely

1 'Obviously there can be no question of a settlement until we have our demands met in full.'

2 'Marriage is plainly on the way out as an institution.'

The speakers of these two sentences are saying that the situation is clear to anybody who knows anything about it. But is it? The words 'obviously' and 'plainly' are being used to prevent further thought. Is it 'obvious' and 'plain' to *everybody*? If so, why does there still appear to be some disagreement? The words suggest that only fools could not agree with the statements.

4.4   Emotive, or coloured language
This is an attempt to influence people by the use of words which appeal to their feelings, or which awaken particular associations.

SAQ 1 _____

The word 'golden' is often used in advertisements. Write down associations people might make with the word 'gold'.

Discussion _____

SAQ 2 _____

Match the association with the word designed to elicit it (e.g. by drawing a line, as in the example given).

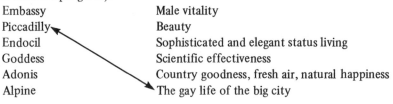

Discussion _____

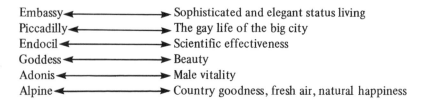

Certain words and images conjure up associations that move us to conclusions almost without thinking about them. A picture of a breakfast cereal is followed by a shot of lush green fields and then a happy family splashing in the stream. The name of the product then becomes associated with a whole series of vital and happy experiences: the implication is that the product will itself bring about these experiences for us.

This technique operates not only in advertising, but also in argument.

SAQ 3

Read the following examples. Each shows an emotive use of language.

- Write down the emotive word or words.

- Say what associations you think they are intended to evoke.

1 'Scab!'

2 'These militants have the economy by the throat.'

3 'Today's youth are a bunch of ill-mannered louts.'

4 'Just another example of the gutter press exploiting people's ignorance.'

Discussion

1 'Scab' has associations of unsightly and painful sores.

2 'Militants' seems less emotive than 'scab', but it is increasingly used as a word to conjure up images of irresponsible violence. The phrase 'by the throat' suggests a predatory animal seizing its helpless victim (e.g. a fox and chicken).

3 'Lout' is a loaded word, conveying thoughtless, insensitive behaviour.

4 'Gutter' – a dirty, unsavoury part of the environment.

SAQ 4

Look back to the statements as given in Self-Assessment Question 3. Rewrite each in more measured, reasonable language.

Discussion

1 'You are failing to support our cause. Stay on our side of the picket line.'

2 'By following policies that involve direct confrontation, these trade unionists are putting the economy under very great pressure.'

3 'Today's young people are ill-mannered.'

4 'The popular press works on the assumption that its readers are ill-informed.'

You will have noticed that the statements become quite different once the emotive words are cut out. When rewritten they lose all their force. They are not really trying to carry forward an argument, but serve to indicate an attitude or prejudice. Their tone is not that of reason; instead of using argument they are throwing abuse. Abuse may be justified on occasions but we must be very careful not to mistake abuse for argument, whether we are using it ourselves or hearing it used by others. Many people think that they are offering argument when all that they are really doing is abusing their opponent. Abuse is often the resort of people who are too tired or frustrated or angry to use proper argument.

Assignment D

Part 1
Read the passage carefully and then answer the questions printed underneath it.

Sir,
What's happened to this once great country of ours? There is little evidence left that we were once the greatest Empire in history.
Our young people certainly give us cause for concern, and surely a country's youth is an important barometer of its health. Take dress as a case in point. Everybody wears the same dreary uniform — jeans and sweatshirt. These are really working clothes but now they are being worn as decoration, just as safety pins are worn as earrings. The whole idea is to shock ordinary decent people with outlandish dress and behaviour.
Music is supposed to be a soothing influence on Man. But our young people gyrate to the electric guitar, in a sexually suggestive manner, to jungle rhythms.
Coloured lights and excessive noise are designed to drive the audience up into a frenzy so that normal, decent standards of behaviour are forgotten. It is well known among behavioural scientists that too much noise can make people behave in irrational ways and when people become irrational they can become dangerous.
The manners of the young today leave a great deal to be desired. They swagger about the streets and act as if the world was their oyster. School-children create havoc when they use public transport and I know of people who prefer to walk rather than to risk the hazards of using the train. Gone are the days when young people would help old ladies across the street or give an elderly person a seat when a bus was crowded.
Look at the graffiti on the walls of our public buildings — no one can deny that this is primarily the grotesque work of the louts. The real problem is that education has thrown in the sponge; the schools are far too soft with young people and what is needed is a return to good old fashioned discipline.
Yours etc...

Questions

1 What examples of emotive language can you find in this passage? If you are unsure about a particular example, say why.

2 Can you find any examples of unreasonable assertions? Write them down.

3 Could you rephrase the arguments of the last paragraph in more measured language?

Keep your answers until you complete this unit.

4.5 Generalisation

1 'All shop stewards are power hungry.'

2 'All landladies are suspicious.'

A generalisation is a general notion or statement based on only a few instances. It makes a universal claim, and is often used disparagingly. The generalisation is very similar to the assertion in that it nearly always requires supporting evidence. Like the assertion, the generalisation can be reasonable or unreasonable. (Check back to the unit on assertions: much that's there is applicable to generalisations too.)

One of us was reading a book about the First World War *(History of the Great European War; Its Causes and Effects,* Vol 5 p. 139, by W. Stanley Macbean Knight, London Caxton Publishing Co. Ltd. and came across a photograph of German prisoners of war entering a compound. The caption read

A careful study of the faces of many of these German soldiers will show that they present aspects of an unmistakably 'degenerate' type; they contrast badly with the keen alert British soldier. All bear their misfortunes with a certain air of enjoyment and no doubt relief.

(Presumably the author means by this last sentence that the soldiers are relieved to be out of the front line of fighting.)

SAQ 5 _____

1 How many generalisations can you spot in the caption?

2 How justifiable are they?

Discussion _____

1 We can spot three.
   a) German soldiers are degenerate.
   b) British soldiers are keen and alert.
   c) German soldiers are cowards and glad to be out of the war.

The implication is that there are racial types; the British are superior and the Germans inferior.

2 The author does admittedly tone down his generalisations by adding 'many', but it is not possible by looking at the photograph to study 'many' faces. We can see clearly the faces of only a few. As for the second generalisation, there are only four British soldiers pictured, and these are visible only in profile.

Just as we all have to use assertions so it is only fair to say that on occasions we all have to make generalisations. If everybody had to give evidence and examples for everything they said or wrote then we would never get anywhere. Many generalisations are quite reasonable; they state what would be widely agreed:

1 'You should wear warm clothes in the English winter.'

2 'Scottish winters are harder than those in Cornwall.'

These are reasonable generalisations, on non-controversial topics. Many proverbs come into this category, too — e.g.

1 'Many a slip 'twixt cup and lip.'

2 'Too many cooks spoil the broth.'

Generalisations of this kind show our ability as human beings to organise experience, to seek out its predictable aspects and to classify events and sensations so that we may live more easily in our environment.

But generalisations should always be treated carefully:

1 in academic work (e.g. essays),
2 when the subject is controversial.

In the street it may be perfectly all right to assert that 'Scottish winters are harder than those in Cornwall', but if we were writing an essay on climate then we would probably need

• to quote evidence (e.g. in this case, temperature figures)
• to show caution (e.g. by using a phrase such as 'tend to' or 'might be expected to be').

We have tried, in this section, to encourage you to beware of generalisations in certain contexts. Ask yourself, in your own speaking and (particularly) in your writing:

• have I made any generalisations?
• if I have, then are they reasonable?
• should I qualify them to make them more tentative?
• do I need to produce *evidence*, and if so, what *kind* of evidence?

Assignment D

Part 2

Complete the following exercise and keep your answer by you since you will be sending it to your tutor at the end of your work on this unit.

Read the following passage and answer the two questions printed beneath it.

> The working class suffered dreadfully during the Industrial Revolution and they bore the entire cost of that transition from an idyllic rural economy to a modern capitalist one.

1 How many generalisations can you see here?

2 Can you modify these (e.g. by including extra words such as 'tend to', or 'possibly')?

3 Can you identify one example of emotive language. Why is it being used here?

Keep your answer, with those to Part 1, until you complete this unit.

4.6 Analogy

This is the name given to the process of reasoning from one set of circumstances or characteristics to another set that is, or seems, similar. Here is an example

- 'The car is like the human body. It must be given proper care and maintenance or it will not function.'

This seems a reasonable enough statement. One can quickly see the relationship between the two: the body has to have nourishing food just as the car has to have well-refined petrol. Other similarities can be drawn — e.g. the car's electrical system might be likened to the body's nervous system.

But we need to look more closely at such an analogy. A good way to test this and similar analogies is to push it to its limits and to look at all aspects of the two things being compared. We can do this by setting out the points in two columns.

✓ or X or ?	CAR	BODY
✓	Fuel	Food
? Nervous system is more complex?	Electrical system	Nervous system
✓	Servicing helps smooth functioning and helps prevent breakdown	Regular medical checks help prevent illness
X	No 'mind'	Is affected by mental/emotional/spiritual factors
X	Needs a driver	Is self-motivating.

An analogy can be an illuminating way of writing or describing things. It opens up an enquiry into two things (in this case the car and the human body) and we could learn more about each of these. An analogy is like a mirror that you hold up and the reflection throws back impressions of the object you are considering. Let us see how this works in a further example.

SAQ 6

• 'Monopoly capitalism is like a pond where trout and perch are forced to live with pike. '

1 What is the pond analogous with?

2 What are pike analogous with?

3 What are trout and perch analogous with?

4 Is this a good analogy? Give reasons for your view.

Discussion

1 Modern capitalist society.

2 Large scale capitalists who gobble up other capitalists as pike gobble up other fish.

3 Small-scale capitalists, e.g. those running small businesses, and employees.

4 We think that this could be considered a good analogy for the following reasons.
   a) Pike are voracious and are known to eat other fish or even their own young. Monopoly capitalism is voracious, and grows by taking over smaller companies.
   b) Trout also eat each other even though they are the weaker fry in the pond. They are analogous with the ordinary people in monopoly capitalist society who could be said to be in competition with one another.

The value of this analogy is that it makes a complex and abstract concept (monopoly capitalism) comprehensible and manageable by comparing it to fish in a pond – something concrete and within the direct experience of everyone. Poets often use analogies similarly; to make the abstract vividly concrete and clear, e.g. 'My love is like a red, red rose'.

But analogies do have their weaknesses. They may illuminate, but they also at the same time over-simplify. Presumably one part of the analogy is that the people are exploited as the weaker fish are eaten. But to be eaten is not the same as to be exploited. This analogy also ignores the institutions that might intervene in the process of eating up. The government would presumably prevent the process from reaching the stage where there was only one monopoly capitalist left and all the rest were gobbled up. It is dangerous to compare the natural world with the human; men create institutions which control the more dangerous animal instincts, and men are more sophisticated than fish. Remember our advice given at the beginning of this section; a good way to test analogies is to push them to their limits and to look at all aspects of the two things being compared. If we do not do this we can easily be led to conclude that the two sets of circumstances are alike in *every* respect. Consider the analogy which compares monopoly capitalism to a pond. Draw up a table (as for the car analogy) and see how far it holds.

Assignment D

Part 3

Now look at the following statements and answer the question printed beneath them. Send your answer to your tutor with Parts 1 and 2 as your assignment for this unit.

1 'Yes, I have climbed to the top of the greasy pole.' (Blake on *Disraeli,* pub. Eyre & Spottiswoode, p. 487. Disraeli was the first Jew to become prime minister.)

2 'This strike will cut the nation's jugular vein.' (James Callaghan)

3 'The best thing to do with capitalist society is to wipe the slate clean.' (Lenin)

How effective are these analogies? What are their limitations? If you wish, you can set out your answer in two columns as we have in the above car/body example.

5. Suspect types of argument: 2

5.1 Introduction

In Unit 4 we looked at

- persuader words
- emotive language
- generalisations
- analogies.

In this unit we continue our look at different types of argument, and we consider

- familiar appeals
- conflation
- rhetorical questions
- syllogisms.

5.2 Familiar Appeals

People often quote 'arguments' which are really ways of avoiding the need to find proper arguments in support of a proposition. We mention three of these in this section. They are really more *appeals* than arguments.

5.2.1 Appeal to the past or to tradition

1 'We've always done it this way.'

2 'If it was good enough for my father then it's good enough for me.'

This kind of 'argument' is a way of avoiding a hard look at the practice or custom under discussion. It's very common, but on its own is scarcely an 'argument' as we define it in the early units of this course.

5.2.2 Appeal to authority

1 'It must be right; it was in last week's *Sunday Times.*'

2 'Jean's husband says so, and he's a doctor.'

3 'Malcolm Smith Ph.D., Professor of Biology at Cambridge University, gives it as his opinion that the British political system will not last another thirty years in its present form.'

SAQ 1 _____

What criticisms would you make of the above three statements, as arguments?

Discussion

1 *The Sunday Times* is not infallible, even though it may have a good reputation for accurate reporting. A lot would depend on whether it was being quoted for its opinion or for its facts — though even facts need careful checking, as we shall see in the next Self-Assessment Question.

2 Again, the appeal to authority begs the question. Is what Jean's husband says reasonable and well-argued? Is he talking about a topic he's expert in?

3 The expertise of Dr. Smith is in Biology. He's talking about politics and may know no more about that than you or me.

SAQ2

We mention above that newspapers are fallible. We reproduce below several items from a range of newspapers reporting an incident in Belfast on April 17th, 1972. Read the following extracts and see if you can establish the main differences between them.

1 The *Belfast Telegraph* on the following day, 18 April, gave this report:

An RUC spokesman said that one confirmed death was that of a student teacher Joseph Magee (20) from Downpatrick who died during a gun battle between troops and terrorists in the Lower Falls yesterday afternoon . . . although the army insist that the student teacher Magee was a gunman, residents and a priest allege that he was merely sheltering from the gunfire when killed.

2 The *Irish Press* in Dublin on 18 April gave this version:

Fierce gun battles between the British Army and the IRA raged throughout Belfast yesterday, and late last night the casualty figure stood at three soldiers shot, two IRA men killed, three wounded and others probably hit, and a nine year old boy shot in the stomach when he was caught in the crossfire.

3 The *Financial Times* in London on the same day, 18 April, gave this version:

In Belfast the army claimed that in an exchange of fire in the Divis Street area two IRA Men were killed.

4 And the *Daily Mirror* in London this version:

Troops said that all the men killed and injured in the battle in riot-scarred Divis Street were gunmen.

5 The *News Letter* in Belfast carried the following headlines on pages 1 and 2 respectively:
ONE SNIPER KILLED BY ARMY

TWO SNIPERS SHOT DEAD AS TERROR ESCALATES

and reported the incident as follows:

The toll in casualties is still uncertain but at midnight it was known officially that several snipers had been wounded and that at least one terrorist had been shot dead.

6.00 Confirmation on one death and three injuries to terrorists in Divis battle.

6 *The Daily Telegraph* in London gave this version:

SNIPER SHOT IN STREET
One gunman was shot dead and three others wounded in fierce street fighting in the Divis Flats area of Belfast yesterday. The army believed they had killed another gunman.

7 *The Guardian* in London gave this version:

A pitched battle raged only a few hundred yards from the centre of Belfast yesterday afternoon as the IRA poured a hail of machine-gun and other small arms fire at army positions in and around Divis Street. The battle was still going on last night by which time two civilians who the army claimed were snipers had been shot dead by the army. Three other civilians were admitted to hospital with gunshot wounds.

(Source of extracts: Open University Course PE 261 Units 8 and 9; *Printed Media and the Reader,* pp. 62-3)

Discussion _____

The main differences are in the reports of the number of men killed and who these men were.

Extract 1 — 1 death, a student teacher aged 20.
    "   2 — 5 deaths, 3 soldiers and 2 I.R.A. men.
    "   3 — 2 deaths, both I.R.A. men.
    "   4 — ? deaths, 'gunmen'.
    "   5 — 1 or 2 deaths, 'snipers'.
    "   6 — 1 death, a 'gunman'.
    "   7 — 2 deaths, 'snipers'.

To compare newspaper accounts will often produce results like this, and should caution us never to accept uncritically what we read. Even 'the facts' may differ from report to report.

5.2.3 Appeal to cost
The cost of something is often quoted as a reason for not doing it. It is one thing to cost something objectively and to decide after due consideration that it is too

expensive. It is quite another to use the question of cost as a way of avoiding all analysis or argument.

The N.H.S. is already costing £8 billion each year. The proposal to introduce widespread screening is going to cost too much and will be the final straw.

5.2.4 Conclusion

Be alert to these appeals — to tradition, to authority and to cost — and ask yourself whether they are being used as ways of avoiding more serious and considered argument.

5.3 Conflation

So far we have looked at types of argument which are relatively easy to detect and to isolate, even though some may not be so easy to cope with. Conflation is a type of argument which is more difficult to find, and so is not always easy to challenge.

Conflation is the 'fusing together of two variant texts. . .into one' (Concise *Oxford Dictionary*, 5th Edition). For our purposes, we can say that it means the fusing or merging together of two ideas or concepts.

Supposing, for example, that we wanted to convince you that the government should not restrict advertising. You would be unlikely to accept this assertion without the provision of some further evidence. We could, however, state

Advertising makes us aware of the greater choices open to us in disposing of our incomes and this habit of exercising choice is of crucial importance when we have to think about politics and elect governments. Advertising is an important bulwark of democracy, and it should not be interfered with.

Two concepts are run together here.

1 Economic choice.

2 Our ability to think about politics and choose a government (i.e. political choice).

The key word is the linking word 'and' ('. . . .disposing of our incomes *and* this habit. . . .'). This draws the two ideas together and thus makes you bridge the gap from economic choice to political choice and to relate both to the necessity for unrestricted advertising.

This fusion of two concepts is often not intentional — an important reason why we want you to learn to detect 'conflation' is so that you can avoid it. What often happens is that people move from one phrase to another which appears to be synonymous.

How can you deal with this form of argument?

1 You look for the linking word (often this is 'and' or 'or'). This is the point at

which the two ideas or concepts are fused.

2 Separate the ideas which have been fused, and ask questions about them — e.g. in the above example, what other things as well as economic choice could guarantee democracy?

SAQ3

Read the following letter to a council house tenant and answer the questions printed beneath it.

Dear Madam,
The Council at its meeting of the 21st April discussed the Inspector's report on the condition of the house occupied by you. It was his opinion that your house is in an 'untidy or filthy condition' — his exact words. We have no alternative but to ask you to start looking for alternative accommodation.

Yours etc. . . .

1 Make a note of that part of the letter where the conflation occurs, i.e. look for a word or phrase which is nearly, but not quite, similar to another word or phrase.

2 Write a letter to the council stating why you think they could be expected to re-examine the Inspector's Report.

Discussion

1 'untidy or filthy'. This illustrates how easily one might fall into a trap. The inspector might have confused 'untidiness' with 'filth' and a responsible authority would certainly want to look further into the matter. Once the word 'filth' is used the image is stronger and more damaging to the unfortunate tenant.

2 We leave this to you!

Watch out for examples of *conflation* in your reading.

Assignment E
Part 1
Read the following extract and answer the questions printed beneath it.

Hitler knows that he will have to break us in this island or lose the war. If we can stand up to him all Europe may be free and the life of the world may move forward into broad sunlit uplands. (Winston Churchill, Speech to the Nation in 1940.)

Questions

1 Where does the conflation occur?

2 What two ideas are being fused?

3 Are there examples of emotive language?

If so, quote them and say what you think the speaker hoped to achieve by using them.

Keep your answers until you finish this unit.

5.4 Rhetorical questions

A rhetorical question is a type of argument stated in the form of a question in such a way that one answer only is possible. The person to whom the question is addressed is compelled to answer as expected. Let's look at an example.

A speaker presenting the case for a better deal for senior citizens states

● 'When are we going to give the old folks of this country the pension they deserve?'

The expected answer that the audience might inwardly give would be 'now' or 'it is high time'. (Notice here as well as the rhetorical question there is a use of emotive language, 'old folks'.)

SAQ4 _____

A person arguing in favour of safety helmets for all riders says

● 'Why should we permit motor cyclists to ignore a law passed for their own protection?'

What is the answer expected here?

Discussion _____

The expected answer is that we should not. Notice that this is not a real question; the speaker knows the answer all the time. He is asking only for agreement, and would be thrown off his guard if someone treated it as a real question and answered genuinely.

SAQ5 _____

● 'Surely we do not need a licence for such a well-behaved pet?'

1 What is the expected answer here?

2 Is there any other type of argument in use here?

Discussion

1 The expected answer is 'No'.

2 The other type of argument is the persuader word — 'surely'. If you've forgotten this, look back to Section 1 of Unit 4. Persuader words and rhetorical questions are similar in that they put pressure on the listener to agree.

A disarming feature of the rhetorical question is that because the person to whom it is addressed makes the expected response he could imagine that he has drawn the conclusion for himself, whereas he has simply walked in through the door opened for him.

5.5 Syllogisms

A syllogism is what happens if we take two premises (or assumptions), put them together, and draw a conclusion — one that is not always sound. Let's look at an example.

1 *First premise:*   Dark circles under the eyes are a sign of loose living.

2 *Second premise:*   Jones has dark circles under his eyes.

3 *Conclusion:*   Therefore Jones must be living a loose life.

With this type of argument we move close to logic, and this isn't a logic course. The important thing to note here is that the conclusion of a syllogism flows from the premises and is usually, but not necessarily, prefaced by the word 'Therefore. . .'.

SAQ 6

What conclusion would you draw from the following two premises?

1 All women like football.

2 Beth is a woman.

3 Therefore Beth likes football.

Discussion

Therefore Beth likes football.

SAQ 7

How would you attack or question this argument?

Discussion

The first premise is an assertion and a generalisation and is unsound. Some women do not like football; you would have to find only one woman who did not like football and the premise would collapse.

From this example we see that it may be necessary to examine the premise of syllogisms to see if they are sound. Since the conclusion follows from the premises then we can destroy the argument by demolishing one of the premises. Like the persuader word and the rhetorical question the syllogism too invites us to draw the conclusion for ourselves and can give us an illusory sense of having participated in a sound argument.

Our discussion of the syllogism concludes our look at types of argument. In Units 4 and 5 we have looked at

- persuader words
- emotive language
- generalisations
- analogies
- familiar appeals
- conflation
- rhetorical questions
- syllogisms.

Assignment E

Part 2

The following passage contains some of the above types of argument. Read it several times and answer the questions beneath it.

Ladies and Gentlemen,

The fad for change which is now gripping this country must not be allowed to spread to our democratic institutions – the House of Commons and the House of Lords.

The attack on the Lords is a good example of new-fangled thinking, but let us hope that this is just another of the many assaults the Lords has had to face in its long and noble history.

I am aware that the Lords is often accused of being unrepresentative because it is non-elected, but it is precisely because it is not elected that it is such a useful and dependable institution. After all, we do live in a pluralist society where all manner of interests – financial, economic, political – have to be represented and an aristocracy surely has as much right to be represented as any other interest group.

The fact of the matter is that society is essentially a conservative institution. Obviously, if we had not given our institutions time to evolve gradually and mellow properly, we would not have such a free and tolerant political climate with clearly defined civil rights and a minimum of political abuse. Evolution is natural to all species, but man seems to be the only species which is always attempting to tamper with the natural order and to control rather than live with nature. Each species in the animal kingdom has leaders and the others are quite content to obey. Even in the insect world this rule applies. Ants and bees, for example, have highly sophisticated social systems and even class structures with leaders, and strict obedience to the needs of the whole group is demanded. Man, however, with his usual arrogance, wants to go against Natural Law and there is no doubt that he has suffered and will continue to suffer for it.

When will we learn that rapid change leads to instability? Instability undermines the foundations of our political structure and the consequences will inevitably be political anarchy. Pragmatism is the concomitant of Conservatism.

Questions

1 Find the proposition and restate it in the simplest language.

2 Prepare an outline of the argument organised beneath the proposition.

3 Point to any assertions/generalisations which should not go unchallenged.

4 Can you find an example of conflation? Explain, in your own words, how the conflation operates.

5 Can you find any examples of

- persuader words
- emotive language
- analogies
- rhetorical questions
- familiar appeals
- syllogisms

What effect might the writer hope to achieve by using these?

6 Looking at your notes for questions (1) – (5) write a balanced criticism of the argument in about 400 words. By 'balanced' we mean that your answer should include a concern with structure, organisation and content.

Send your answers to all 6 questions to your tutor together with those to Part 1.

5.6 Conclusion
To finish with, we want to add further notes on three other aspects of how to conduct a good argument.

5.6.1 Content
We have concentrated a great deal in this course on the structure of arguments as

we feel that this gives students and others the greatest difficulties. It is not easy either to spot the structural weaknesses in the arguments of others or to organise a coherently structured argument of one's own. We hope that our method will have helped.

You should also, of course, always look at the *content* of the arguments offered. Do they make sense? Are they clear? Do they match your own experience of life?

5.6.2 Ending constructively

If you are presenting an argument of your own, try to get into the habit of developing a good clear outline, and if you wish to use the types of argument we have discussed in Units 4 and 5 then try to impose these on a sound structure.

Aim at all times for a clear statement of the proposition, test every argument for relevance, and try to end your argument on a constructive note, especially if you have been criticising some other party, person or body of ideas. Emotive and persuasive language very often has a negative effect and is unlikely to be constructive.

5.6.3 Tone

Very often, as we said in Unit 1, the tone of argument becomes heated or aggressive. This is unfortunate as it makes the argument 'personal' and deflects attention from the structure and content of the case put forward. Very often an unemotional and impartial tone carries more weight with an audience.

SAQ 8 _____

Look back at the following two arguments.

1   Unit 4, Assignment D, Part 1; the passage on today's youth.

2   Unit 2, Self-Assessment Question 2; the passage on microprocessors.

Re-read these two passages.

Which one seems to you closer to the ideal of tone which we have just outlined? Give reasons for your view.

Discussion _____

The passage from Unit 2 is far calmer and more dispassionate. There's an absence of emotive language. It uses cautious words like 'fairly', and there's no simple political line being taken. The writer seems to be thinking as he writes.

The passage on today's youth, on the other hand, is impatient and bullying. The writer uses emotive words and seems to be basing his argument on stereotypes. The use of assertions (some unreasonable) is typical of an argument conducted in this tone.

You may like to look at other passages quoted in the course from the point of view of their tone.

6.Summary

6.1 Introduction

In this unit we want to pull together the course and give you some practice in working on a substantial passage in a variety of ways, to evaluate the structure and content of its argument.

Assignment F

Read the following passage carefully, several times. Then work through the questions printed beneath it and write answers to each in note form. Then write your notes up into continuous prose and send this evaluation to your tutor.

The Virtues of Advertising

Why it is that so many pseudo-intellectuals and left-wingers take such a delight in attacking advertising? Surely these people are typical of a brand of politicians who hate to see the ordinary man in the street getting a kick out of life because, let's face it, advertising has the saving grace of bringing the good things of life to the notice of the people.

Those long-haired kill-joys forget that in the world of industry there is obviously a crying need for information about products; how they work; how they are assembled and so on and, in these days of high technology, advertising performs the task of informing industry and the people extremely well.

The morning paper, that great institution in British life, would probably cost 50 pence if it were not for the fact that advertising subsidises the newspaper industry and, more than this, the widespread advertising of goods in the shops helps to increase sales; and it is well known that increased sales and higher turn- over reduces the prices of goods.

The benefits of advertising are universal. People would still be ignorant of many of the things which improve their living standard, e.g. motor cars and vacuum cleaners. The shopkeeper has the advantage of a high volume of sales which reduces prices and keeps his capital turning over, and it should not go unnoticed that a regular volume of sales ensures that people are kept in work replacing the goods which have been sold because of advertising, and the cost of living is kept down.

There are even more powerful arguments in favour of advertising than the economic ones. Britain, the first industrial nation, has always believed in and practised economic freedom. People have the right to make what they want to make and they have the right to spend their money as they see fit. Advertising helps this process too because the nation's goods are brought to the nation's attention and the choice is more meaningful because it is based upon a lot of information. We would tamper with this right at our peril, because once you remove the freedom to spend money as the owner sees fit then the whole institution of private property is threatened and with that the basis of democratic life goes too.

Advertising has also promoted an increase in cultural standards in this country. Our independent television channel (which incidentally costs the people nothing) brings to our life a magnificent range of films, plays, news programmes, political coverage, not to mention music — how unrewarding our lives would be without this.

It is worth noting that advertisers rarely defend themselves against the critics and the reason for this is simple; they know the worth of the contribution they make to our way of life and they know that no matter what the moralists and so-called intellectuals might say, advertising is an institution which has earned its place and which will survive those who denigrate it.

Questions

1   What is the proposition?

2   What are the arguments? Divide each into topic and point.

3   Are any arguments repeated?

4   Does the argument develop logically?

5   Does each argument relate to and try to prove the proposition?

6   Are there any assertions? Do these need to be changed? E.g. by the provision of further evidence, or by the addition of words to indicate caution?

7   If the argument is criticising something then does it end constructively?

8   Are there any examples of
    a) persuader words?
    b) emotive language?
    c) generalisations?
    d) analogies?
    e) familiar appeals?
    f) conflation?
    g) rhetorical questions?
    h) syllogisms?

9   If so, comment on their use.

10 Which arguments convince you? Explain the flaws in those which do not.

6.2   Poetry

The method outlined in this course can also be used when trying to come to terms with poetry and prose. We try to demonstrate this in the following example.

Read the following poem several times and write notes in answer to the questions printed beneath it.

Dulce et Decorum Est
Bent double, like old beggars under sacks,
Knock-kneed, coughing like hags, we cursed through sludge,
Till on the haunting flares we turned our backs,
And towards our distant rest began to trudge.
Men marched asleep. Many had lost their boots,
But limped on, blood-shod. All went lame, all blind;
Drunk with fatigue; deaf even to the hoots
Of gas-shells dropping softly behind.

Gas! GAS! Quick boys! – An ecstasy of fumbling.
Fitting the clumsy helmets just in time,
But someone still was yelling out and stumbling
And floundering like a man in fire or lime. –
Dim through the misty panes and thick green light,
As under a green sea, I saw him drowning.

In all my dreams before my helpless sight,
He plunges at me, guttering, choking, drowning.

If in some smothering dreams, you too could pace
Behind the wagon that we flung him in,
And watch the white eyes writhing in his face,
His hanging face, like a devil's sick of sin;
If you could hear, at every jolt, the blood
Come gargling from the froth-corrupted lungs,
Bitter as the cud
Of vile, incurable sores on innocent tongues, –
My friend, you would not tell with such high zest
To children ardent for some desperate glory,
The old Lie: *Dulce et decorum est*
Pro patria mori.
(Wilfred Owen, *Dulce et Decorum Est*)

1 What do you think the author is trying to prove (i.e. what is his proposition)?

2 What arguments does he use to prove it? Give the topic and point of each if you can.

3 Is there any emotive language? If so, is it justified?

You may also like to have a go at describing the structure of the poem; how the poet built it up.

Discussion

1 The proposition – that war is a horrible thing and that people shouldn't disguise this – runs through the whole poem. The Latin title is part of a line written by the poet Horace – *Dulce et decorum est pro patria mori:* 'it is sweet and fitting to die for one's country'. The poem seeks to disprove this statement, pointing out that death in warfare is neither sweet nor fitting.

2 a) The topic of the argument of the first stanza is the soldiers returning from a patrol. The point (what is said about the soldiers) is that they are tired, coughing, ill-shod, lame, blind, deaf. Notice the repetition, for example of lameness and fatigue. This is used to poetic effect, deliberately to emphasise the men's desperation.

b) The topic of the second stanza is the soldiers' experience of a gas attack. The point: they are trying to get their helmets on and at least one doesn't succeed. He is yelling out and floundering. Notice the poetic analogies: 'Like a man in fire or lime'; 'as under a green sea'.
(The idea is repeated, separated for effect, in the two lines that follow the stanza.)

c) The third main stanza (beginning 'If in some smothering dreams. . . .') describes the dying man. The details of his agony form the point, and they lead to a final explicit statement of the proposition, with a direct address to the reader.

3 Yes, throughout. In a poem of this kind emotive language (provided it is controlled) is certainly justified. In this it is different from a rational prose argument.

The structure of the poem is like this.

The first stanza presents a picture: the poet is talking about himself and others (*'We* cursed through sludge . . . .*we* turned *our* backs. . . . .'). In the second stanza he takes us right into the centre of a particular experience *as if it is happening in the present,* 'Gas! GAS! Quick, boys!' and then gives us his reflections on what he saw in that frightening experience. He tries to make it real to us by using analogies – i.e. by relating this experience of war (which we *don't* have, sitting at home) to experiences which we *can* perhaps imagine (e.g. the rather horrible one in stanza 3 of chewing a tongue covered with sores). The poet then suddenly steps out of the situation and addresses us. It turns out that *we* have been guilty of speaking the Latin tag: the poem is trying to persuade *us* how wrong we are. The tone changes to that of debate.

We are accused of deception and ignorance.

We offer this as *one* way of coming to terms with a poem, a way we've found works successfully with students otherwise uncertain of where to start. It is important not to apply the method too rigorously and to remember that poems generally (and this one in particular) are trying to make an emotional impact rather than to establish a rational argument. Nevertheless in a fine poem the language is carefully constructed to achieve this impact, and the poet is using his intellect as well as his emotions. Thus a good poem is put together as carefully as any good prose argument, though it uses different means. It does thus offer a kind of 'argument'.

6.3   Suggestions for extra work

1   If you are studying (or will soon be studying) a course including literature you could choose a poem or a piece of prose and analyse it in the way that we have just outlined.

2   Look through newspapers and periodicals and try to find an argument which you consider is either particularly good or particularly bad. Provide an analysis of the argument in the way suggested in this course. Make sure that you consider the *structure* of the argument, as well as its content.

If you choose to undertake this extra work you can send it to your tutor, but if you do this then please make sure that you also send him a copy of the original source (e.g. the poem, piece of prose, or article from the newspaper).

7. Source material

7.1 Introduction

This is a fairly lengthy exercise in which we hope to get you to try out your skills in thinking and writing. You will have to read pieces of evidence from a variety of sources, to sort these out in your mind and then you will have to write an essay.

The best way to proceed is to adopt the method we have been proposing throughout this course. Start from the assumption that each writer had something that he wanted to prove and prepare a brief outline with a statement of the proposition (as far as you are able to detect it) and an outline of the arguments. When you have done this you will have a set of notes and from these notes we want you to try to answer an essay question. We want you to use the same method when you set out your essay – i.e. to try to make a clear statement of what *you* are trying to prove and then to build up your arguments, paragraph by paragraph.

The topic is 'Industrialisation and its effect on the British working class'. This has been the subject of long-running controversy over many years; enough books have been written about it to fill a library. You are not being asked to do any reading other than that provided for you, and of course we do not pretend that this will give you anything other than a superficial knowledge of a very complex topic.

We suggest that you work through the following stages. Read through these first, and then return to carry out the work suggested at each stage.

1 Think about the question you will be answering. This is:
  'The Industrial Revolution was a disaster for the British working class.' Do you agree or disagree with this assertion? Give reasons for your view.

2 Read through all the passages.

3 Prepare a set of notes for each passage, to include a statement of what seems to be the proposition and what arguments are being used to support it. You might also organise the evidence into the categories of 'agree' and 'disagree' with the question.

4 Read the question and the notes you make at stage 3, and think about the subject for a day or so.

5 Decide what your proposition is, and state it clearly. This is very important.

6 Organise your arguments to try to prove this proposition. We suggest that you do this in outline form first, experimenting to find the best sequence of arguments.

7 Check to see whether your arguments contain any assertions or any other of the forms of argument discussed in Units 3, 4 and 5. Do you need to rephrase any of your points, or to find more evidence from the passages to support what you say?

8 Make a rough copy of your answer, which should be about 500—700 words long. If you write more, then that is fine; but make sure that your organisation is clear. You will probably feel that you are lacking information. Again we remind you that the challenge is to use what is provided to the full. Your tutor is well aware of the limited nature of your material and he will take that into account when he marks your essay.

9 Read your rough draft carefully, and make any changes you think necessary. In particular check:
   a) that you start with a clear statement of your proposition;
   b) that you choose relevant arguments and organise them to the best effect;
   c) that your expression is as accurate and exact as you can get it.

10 Then copy up your corrected rough draft and send it to your tutor as your assignment for this unit.

7.2. Sources: Assignment G

Source 1

The Industrial Environment

Coketown, to which Messrs Bounderby and Gradgrind now walked, was a triumph of fact; it had no greater taint of fancy in it than Mrs Gradgrind herself. Let us strike the keynote, Coketown, before pursuing our tune.

It was a town of red brick, or of brick that would have been red if the smoke and ashes had allowed it; but as matters stood it was a town of unnatural red and black like the painted face of a savage. It was a town of machinery and tall chimneys, out of which interminable serpents of smoke trailed themselves for ever and ever, and never got uncoiled. It had a black canal in it, and a river that ran purple with ill-smelling dye, and vast piles of buildings full of windows where there was a rattling and a trembling all day long, and where the piston of the steam-engine worked monotonously up and down like the head of an elephant in a state of melancholy madness. It contained several large streets all very like one another, and many small streets still more like one another, inhabited by people equally like one another, who all went in and out at the same hours, with the same sound upon the same pavements, to do the same work, and to whom every day was the same as yesterday and to-morrow, and every year the counterpart of the last and the next.

These attributes of Coketown were in the main inseparable from the work by which it was sustained; against them were to be set off, comforts of life which found their way all over the world, and elegancies of life which made, we will not ask how much of the fine lady, who could scarcely bear to hear the place mentioned. The rest of its features were voluntary, and they were these.

You saw nothing in Coketown but what was severely workful. If the members of a religious persuasion built a chapel there — as the members of eighteen religious persuasions had done — they made it a pious warehouse of red brick, with sometimes (but this is only in highly ornamental examples) a bell in a bird-cage on the top of it. The solitary exception was the New Church; a stuccoed edifice with a square steeple over the door, terminating in four short pinnacles like florid wooden legs. All the public inscriptions in the town were painted alike, in severe characters of black and white. The jail might have been the infirmary, the infirmary might have been the jail, the town-hall might have been either, or both, or anything else, for anything that appeared to the contrary in the graces of their construction. Fact, fact, fact, everywhere in the material aspect of the town; fact, fact, fact, everywhere in the immaterial. The M'Choakumchild school was all fact, and the school of design was all fact, and the relations between master and man were all fact, and everything was fact between the lying-in hospital and the cemetery, and what you couldn't state in figures, or show to be purchaseable in the cheapest market and saleable in the dearest, was not, and never should be, world without end, Amen. . . .

A sunny midsummer day. There was such a thing sometimes, even in Coke-town.

Seen from a distance in such weather, Coketown lay shrouded in a haze of its own, which appeared impervious to the sun's rays. You only knew the town was there, because you knew there could have been no such sulky blotch upon the prospect without a town. A blur of soot and smoke, now confusedly tending this way, now that way, now aspiring to the vault of Heaven, now murkily creeping along the earth as the wind rose and fell, or changed its quarter: a dense formless jumble, with sheets of cross light in it, that showed nothing but masses of dark-ness: — Coketown in the distance was suggestive of itself, though not a brick of it could be seen.

The wonder was, it was there at all. It had been ruined so often, that it was amazing how it had borne so many shocks. Surely there never was such fragile china-ware as that of which the millers of Coketown were made. Handle them never so lightly and they fell to pieces with such ease that you might suspect them of having been flawed before. They were ruined when they were required to send labouring children to school; they were ruined when inspectors were appointed to look into their works; they were ruined when such inspectors con-sidered it doubtful whether they were quite justified in chopping people up with their machinery; they were utterly undone, when it was hinted that perhaps they need not always make quite so much smoke. Besides Mr Bounderby's gold spoon which was generally received in Coketown, another prevalent fiction was very popular there. It took the form of a threat. Whenever a Coketowner felt he was ill-used — that is to say, whenever he was not left entirely alone, and it was proposed to hold him accountable for the consequences of any of his acts — he was sure to come out with the awful menace, that he would 'sooner pitch his property into the Atlantic.' This had terrified the Home Secretary within an inch of his life, on several occasions.

However, the Coketowners were so patriotic after all, that they never had pitched their property into the Atlantic yet, but, on the contrary, had been kind enough to take mighty good care of it. So there it was, in the haze yonder; and it increased and multiplied.

The streets were hot and dusty on the summer day, and the sun was so bright that it even shone through the heavy vapour drooping over Coketown, and could not be looked at steadily. Stokers emerged from low underground doorways into factory yards, and sat on steps, and posts, and palings, wiping their swarthy visages, and contemplating coals. The whole town seemed to be frying in oil. There was a stifling smell of hot oil everywhere. The steam-engines shone with it, the dresses of the Hands were soiled with it, the mills throughout their many stories oozed and trickled it. The atmosphere of those Fairy palaces was like the breath of the simoom: and their inhabitants, wasting with heat, toiled languidly in the desert. But no temperature made the melancholy mad elephants more mad or more sane. Their wearisome heads went up and down at the same rate, in hot weather and cold, wet weather and dry, fair weather and foul. The measured motion of their shadows on the walls, was the substitute Coketown had to show for the shadows of rustling woods; while, for the summer hum of insects, it could offer, all the year round, from the dawn of Monday to the night of Saturday, the whirr of shafts and wheels.

Drowsily they whirred all through this sunny day, making the passenger more sleepy and more hot as he passed the humming walls of the mills. Sun-blinds, and sprinklings of water, a little cooled the main streets and the shops; but the mills, and the courts and alleys, baked at a fierce heat. Down upon the river that was black and thick with dye, some Coketown boys who were at large – a rare sight there – rowed a crazy boat, which made a spumous track upon the water as it jogged along, while every dip of an oar stirred up vile smells. But the sun itself, however **beneficent,** generally, was less kind to Coketown than hard frost, and rarely looked intently into any of its closer regions without engendering more death than life.

From Charles Dickens, *Hard Times,* (1854) book i, Chapter 5,
book ii, Chapter 1.

Source 2
A Midland journey

Five-and-thirty years ago the glory had not yet departed from the old coach-roads; the great roadside inns were still brilliant with well-polished tankards, the smiling glances of pretty barmaids, and the repartees of jocose ostlers; the mail still announced itself by the merry notes of the horn; the hedge-cutter or the rick-thatcher might still know the exact hour by the unfailing yet otherwise meteoric apparition of the pea-green Tally-ho or the yellow Independent; and elderly gentlemen in pony-chaises, quartering nervously to make way for the rolling swinging swiftness, had not ceased to remark that times were finely changed since they used to see the pack-horses and hear the tinkling of their bells on this very highway.

In those days there were pocket boroughs, a Birmingham unrepresented in Parliament and compelled to make strong representations out of it, unrepealed corn-laws, three-and-sixpenny letters, a brawny and many-breeding pauperism, and other departed evils; but there were some pleasant things too, which have also departed. *Non omnia grandior aetas quae jugiamus habet,* says the wise goddess: you have not the best of it in all things. O Youngsters! The elderly man has his enviable memories, and not the least of them is the memory of a long journey in mid-spring or autumn on the outside of a stage-coach. Posterity may be shot, like a bullet through a tube, by atmospheric pressure from Winchester to Newcastle; that is a fine result to have among our hopes; but the slow old-fashioned way of getting from one end of our country to the other is the better thing to have in the memory. The tube-journey can never lend much to picture and narrative; it is as barren as an exclamatory O! Whereas the happy outside passenger seated on the box from the dawn to the gloaming gathered enough stories of English life, enough of English labours in town and country, enough aspects of earth and sky, to make episodes for a modern Odyssey. Suppose only that his journey took him through that central plain, watered at one extremity by the Avon, at the other by the Trent. As the morning silvered the meadows with their long lines of bushy willows marking the watercourses, or burnished the golden corn-ricks clustered near the long roofs of some midland homestead, he saw the full-uddered cows driven from their pasture to the early milking. Perhaps it was the shepherd, head-servant of the farm, who drove them, his sheep-dog following with a heedless unofficial air as of a beadle in undress. The shepherd with a slow and slouching walk, timed by the walk of grazing beasts, moved aside, as if unwillingly, throwing out a monosyllabic hint to his cattle; his glance, accustomed to rest on things very near the earth, seemed to lift itself with difficulty to the coachman. Mail or stage coach for him belonged to that mysterious distant system of things called 'Gover'ment,' which, whatever it might be, was no business of his, any more than the most out-lying nebula or the coal-sacks of the southern hemisphere: his solar system was the parish; the master's temper and the casualties of lambing-time were his region of storms. He cut his bread and bacon with his pocket-knife, and felt no bitterness except in the matter of pauper labourers and the bad-luck that sent contrarious seasons and the sheep-rot. He and his cows were soon left behind, and the homestead too, with its pond overhung by elder-trees, its untidy kitchen-garden and cone-shaped yew-tree arbour. But everywhere the bushy hedgerows wasted the land with their straggling beauty, shrouded the grassy borders of the pastures with catkined hazels, and tossed their long blackberry branches on the corn-fields. Perhaps they were white with May, or starred with pale pink dogroses; perhaps the urchins were already nutting amongst them, or gathering the plenteous crabs. It was worth the journey only to see those hedgerows, the liberal homes of unmarketable beauty — of the purple-blossomed ruby-berried night-shade, of the wild convolvulus climbing and spreading in tendrilled strength till it made a great curtain of pale-green hearts and white trumpets, of the many-tubed honey-suckle which, in its most delicate fragrance, hid a charm more subtle and pene-trating than beauty. Even if it were winter the hedgerows showed their coral, the scarlet haws, the deep-crimson hips, with lingering brown leaves to make a resting-place for the jewels of the hoar-frost. Such hedgerows were often as tall as the labourers' cottages dotted along the lanes, or clustered into a small hamlet, their little dingy windows telling, like thick-filmed eyes, of nothing but the darkness within. The passenger on the coach-box, bowled along above such a hamlet, saw chiefly the roofs of it: probably it turned its back on the road, and seemed to lie away from everything but its own patch of earth and sky, away from the parish church by long fields and green lanes, away from all intercourse except that of tramps. If its face could be seen, it was most likely dirty; but the dirt was Protestant dirt, and the big, bold, gin-breathing tramps were Protestant tramps. There was no sign of superstition near, no crucifix or image to indicate a misguided reverence: the inhabitants were probably so free from superstition that they were in much less awe of the parson than of the overseer. Yet they were saved from the excesses of Protestanism by not knowing how to read, and by the absence of handlooms and mines to be the pioneers of Dissent: they were kept safely in the *via media* of indifference, and could have registered themselves in the census by a big black mark as members of the Church of England.

But there were trim cheerful villages too, with a neat or handsome parsonage and grey church set in the midst; there was the pleasant tinkle of the black-smith's anvil, the patient cart-horses waiting at his door; the basket-maker peeling his willow wands in the sunshine; the wheelwright putting the last touch to a blue cart with red wheels; here and there a cottage with bright transparent windows showing pots full of blooming balsams or geraniums, and little gardens in front all double daisies or dark wallflowers; at the well, clean and comely women carrying yoked buckets, and towards the free school small Britons dawdling on, and handling their marbles in the pockets of unpatched corduroys adorned with brass buttons. The land around was rich and marly, great corn-stacks stood in the rick-yards — for the rick-burners had not found their way hither; the homesteads were those of rich farmers who paid no rent, or had the rare advantage of a lease, and could afford to keep their corn till prices had risen. The coach would be sure to overtake some of them on their way to their outlying fields or to the market-town, sitting heavily on their well-groomed horses, or weighing down one side of an olive-green gig. They probably thought of the coach with some contempt, as an accommodation for people who had not their own gigs, or who, wanting to travel to London and such distant places, belonged to the trading and less solid part of the nation. The passenger on the box could see that this was the district of protuberant optimists, sure that old England was the best of all possible countries, and that if there were any facts which had not fallen under their own observation, they were facts not worth observing: the district of clean little market-towns without manufactures, of fat livings, an aristocratic clergy, and low poor-rates. But as the day wore on the scene would change: the land would begin to be blackened with coal-pits, the rattle of handlooms to be heard in hamlets and villages. Here were powerful men walking queerly with knees bent outward from squatting in the mine, going home to throw themselves down in their blackened flannel and sleep through the daylight, then rise and spend much of their high wages at the ale-house with their fellows of the Benefit Club; here the pale eager faces of handloom-weavers, men and women haggard from sitting up late at night to finish the week's work, hardly begun till the Wednesday. Everywhere the cottages and the small children were dirty, for the languid mothers gave their strength to the loom; pious Dissenting women, perhaps, who took life patiently, and thought that salvation depended chiefly on predestination, and not at all on cleanliness. The gables of Dissenting chapels now made a visible sign of religion, and of a meeting-place to counterbalance the ale-house, even in the hamlets; but if a couple of old termagants were seen tearing each other's caps, it was a safe con-clusion that, if they had not received the sacraments of the Church, they had not at least given into schismatic rites, and were free from the errors of Voluntary-ism. The breath of the manufacturing town, which made a cloudy day and a red gloom by night on the horizon, diffused itself over all the surrounding country, filling the air with eager unrest. Here was a population not convinced that old

England was as good as possible; here were multitudinous men and women aware that their religion was not exactly the religion of their rulers, who might therefore be better than they were, and who, if better, might alter many things which now made the world perhaps more painful than it need be, and certainly more sinful. Yet there were the grey steeples too, and the churchyards, with their grassy mounds and venerable headstones, sleeping in the sunlight; there were broad fields and homesteads, and fine old woods covering a rising ground, or stretching far by the roadside, allowing only peeps at the park and mansion which they shut in from the working-day world. In these midland districts the traveller passed rapidly from one phase of English life to another; after looking down on a village dingy with coal-dust, noisy with the shaking of looms, he might skirt a parish all of fields, high hedges, and deep-rutted lanes; after the coach had rattled over the pavement of a manufacturing town, the scene of riots and trades-union meetings, it would take him in another ten minutes into a rural region, where the neighbourhood of the town was only felt in the advantages of a near market for corn, cheese, and hay, and where men with a considerable banking account were accustomed to say that 'they never meddled with politics themselves.' The busy scenes of the shuttle and the wheel, of the roaring furnace, of the shaft and the pulley, seemed to make but crowded nests in the midst of the large-spaced, slow-moving life of homesteads and far-away cottages and oak-sheltered parks. Looking at the dwellings scattered among the woody flats and the ploughed uplands, under the low grey sky which overhung them with an unchanting stillness as if Time itself were pausing, it was easy for the traveller to conceive that town and country had no pulse in common, except where the handlooms made a far-reaching struggling fringe about the great centres of manufacture; that till the agitation about the Catholics in '29, rural Englishmen had hardly known more of Catholics than of the fossil mammals; and that their notion of Reform was a confused combination of rick-burners, trades-unions, Nottingham riots, and in general whatever required the calling-out of the yeomanry. It was still easier to see that, for the most part, they resisted the rotation of crops and stood by their fallows: and the coachman would perhaps tell how in one parish an innovating farmer, who talked of Sir Humphrey Davy, had been fairly driven out by popular dislike, as if he had been a confounded Radical; and how, the parson having one Sunday preached from the words, 'Break up your fallow-ground,' the people thought he had made the text out of his own head, otherwise it would never have come 'so pat' on a matter of business; but when they found it in the Bible at home, some said it was an argument for fallows (else why should the Bible mention fallows?), but a few of the weaker sort were shaken and thought it was an argument that fallows should be done away with, else the Bible would have said, 'Let your fallows lie,' and the next morning the parson had a stroke of apoplexy, which, as coincident with a dispute about fallows, so set the parish against the innovating farmer and the rotation of crops, that he could stand his ground no longer, and transferred his lease.

The coachman was an excellent travelling companion and commentator on the landscape: he could tell the names of sites and persons, and explain the meaning of groups, as well as the shade of Virgil in a more memorable journey; he had as many stories about parishes, and the men and women in them, as the Wanderer in the 'Excursion', only his style was different. His view of life had originally been genial, and such as became a man who was well warmed within and without, and held a position of easy, undisputed authority; but the recent initiation of Railways had embittered him: he now, as in a perpetual vision, saw the ruined country strewn with shattered limbs, and regarded Mr Huskisson's death as a proof of God's anger against Stephenson. 'Why, every inn on the road would be shut up!' and at that word the coachman looked before him with the blank gaze of one who had driven his coach to the outermost edge of the universe, and saw his leaders plunging into the abyss. Still he would soon relapse from the high prophetic strain to the familiar one of narrative. He knew whose the land was wherever he drove; what noblemen had half-ruined themselves by gambling; who made handsome returns of rent; and who was at daggers-drawn with his eldest son. He perhaps remembered the fathers of actual baronets, and knew stories of their extravagant or stingy housekeeping; whom they had married, whom they had horsewhipped, whether they were particular about preserving their game, and whether they had had much to do with canal companies. About any actual landed proprietor he could also tell whether he was a Reformer or an Anti-Reformer. That was a distinction which had 'turned up' in latter times, and along with it the paradox, very puzzling to the coachman's mind, that there were men of old family and large estate who voted for the Bill. He did not grapple with the paradox; he let it pass, with all the discreetness of an experienced theologian or learned scholiast, preferring to point his whip at some object which could raise no questions.

From George Eliot, *'Felix Holt, the Radical'* (1876) Chap. 1

Source 3

**Manchester
2 July 1835**

An undulating plain, or rather a collection of little hills. Below the hills a narrow river (the Irwell), which flows slowly to the Irish sea. Two streams (the Meddlock and the Irk) wind through the uneven ground and after a thousand bends, flow into the river. Three canals made by man unite their tranquil, lazy waters at the same point. On this watery land, which nature and art have contributed to keep damp, are scattered palaces and hovels. Everything in the exterior appearance of the city attests the individual powers of man; nothing the directing power of society. At every turn human liberty shows its capricious creative force. There is no trace of the slow continuous action of government.

Thirty or forty factories rise on the tops of the hills I have just described. Their six stories tower up; their huge enclosures give notice from afar of the centralisation of industry. The wretched dwellings of the poor are scattered haphazard around them. Round them stretches land uncultivated but without the charm of rustic nature, and still without the amenities of a town. The soil has been taken away, scratched and torn up in a thousand places, but it is not yet covered with the habitations of men. The land is given over to industry's use. The roads which connect the still-disjointed limbs of the great city, show, like the rest, every sign of hurried and unfinished work; the incidental activity of a population bent on gain, which seeks to amass gold so as to have everything else all at once, and, in the interval, mistrusts all the niceties of life. Some of these roads are paved, but most of them are full of ruts and puddles into which foot or carriage wheel sinks deep. Heaps of dung, rubble from buildings, putrid, stagnant pools are found here and there among the houses and over the bumpy, pitted surfaces of the public places. No trace of surveyor's rod or spirit level. Amid this noisome labyrinth, this great sombre stretch of brickwork, from time to time one is astonished at the sight of fine stone buildings with Corinthian columns. It might be a medieval town with the marvels of the nineteenth century in the middle of it. But who could describe the interiors of these quarters set apart, home of vice and poverty, which surround the huge palaces of industry and clasp them in their hideous folds. On ground below the level of the river and over-shadowed on every side by immense workshops, stretches marshy land which widely spaced ditches can neither drain nor cleanse. Narrow, twisting roads lead down to it. They are lined with one-story houses whose ill-fitting planks and broken windows show them up, even from a distance, as the last refuge a man might find between poverty and death. None-the-less the wretched people living in them can still inspire jealousy of their fellow-beings. Below some of their miserable dwellings is a row of cellars to which a sunken corridor leads. Twelve to fifteen human beings are crowded pell-mell into each of these damp, repulsive holes.

The fetid, muddy waters, stained with a thousand colours by the factories they pass, of one of the streams I mentioned before, wander slowly round this refuge of poverty. They are nowhere kept in place by quays: houses are built haphazard on their banks. Often from the top of one of their steep banks one sees an attempt at a road opening out through the debris of earth, and the foundations of some houses or the debris of others. It is the Styx of this new Hades. Look up and all around this place and you will see the huge palaces of industry. You will hear the noise of furnaces, the whistle of steam. These vast structures keep air and light out of the human habitations which they dominate; they envelope them in perpetual fog; here is the slave, there the master; there is the wealth of some, here the poverty of most; there the organised efforts of thousands produce, to the profit of one man, what society has not yet learnt to give. Here the weakness of the individual seems more feeble and helpless even than in the middle of a wilderness.

A sort of black smoke covers the city. The sun seen through it is a disc without rays. Under this half-daylight 300,000 human beings are ceaselessly at work. A thousand noises disturb this dark, damp labyrinth, but they are not all the ordinary sounds one hears in great cities.

The footsteps of a busy crowd, the crunching wheels of machinery, the shriek of steam from boilers, the regular beat of the looms, the heavy rumble of carts, those are the noises from which you can never escape in the sombre half-light of these streets. You will never hear the clatter of hoofs as the rich man drives back home or out on expeditions of pleasure. Never the gay shouts of people amusing themselves, or music heralding a holiday. You will never see smart folk strolling at leisure in the streets, or going out on innocent pleasure parties in the surrounding country. Crowds are ever hurrying this way and that in the Manchester streets, but their footsteps are brisk, their looks pre-occupied, and their appearance sombre and harsh. . .

From this foul drain the greatest stream of human industry flows out to fertilise the whole world. From this filthy sewer pure   gold flows. Here humanity attains its most complete development and its most brutish: here civilisation makes its miracles, and civilised man is turned back almost into a savage.

From Alexis de Tocqueville, *'Journeys to England and Ireland'*, trans. G. Lawrence and K.P. Mayer, ed. J.P. Mayer, 1958, pp. 105-8

Source 4
Working Conditions in Scottish Mines

A Royal Commission is the most authoritative of official bodies in the investigation of economic and social problems. Today it tends to be composed in such a way as to give a 'balanced' consideration to its subject. This was not always the case. The famous Commissions on the Poor Law (1832-4), Municipal Corporations (1834-5) and Oxford and Cambridge Universities (1850-2) had their conclusions more or less determined for them by the reforming Whig Governments which appointed them, and were simply intended to expose the expected abuses in the situations they inquired into. There is a greater similarity between them and Chadwick's one-man sanitary report of 1842 than between them and later bodies which bore the same title.

The Commission on the Trades Unions (1867-9) comes at the transitional stage. Pressures from two opposed viewpoints led to its being set up: the unions were campaigning for legal recognition and for the repeal of the 'Master and Servant' laws, which placed the employee at a grave disadvantage in suing or being sued by his employer over breach of contract; and conservatively minded M.P.s, seizing reports of coercion by union officials during a strike at Sheffield as evidence that trade unions were terroristic organisations, wanted to prove that they were. The Commission, however, was not weighted greatly on either side, and eventually recommended the granting of a rather qualified legal recognition to the unions; while a minority report, the work of its most radical members Tom Hughes, author of 'Tom Brown's Schooldays', and Frederic Harrison, urged straightforward legalisation.

Government action followed the report of the Commission in being ambiguous: an Act was passed in 1871 legalising the unions but prohibiting picketing. However, following further agitation and another Commission, the 'Master and Servant' laws and the prohibition of picketing were ended in 1875.

15,252. (*Lord Elcho.*) What year was it in which you entered the mines? – About the year 1835 I think; I could not fix the year. When I entered the mines at eight years of age or so, at that time workings were not so large for we had not sunk in Scotland to the thicker seams which are now being worked.

15,253. What mine did you enter? – A mine called the Dyke Head Ironstone Mine.

15,254. Not a coal mine? – Not a coal mine at first.

15,255. Where is that mine? – In Lanarkshire.

15,256. Does that mine still exist? – It does not exist now, it has long since been closed. The condition of the miner's boy then was to be raised about 1 o'clock or 2 o'clock in the morning if the distance was very far to travel, and I at that time had to travel a considerable distance, more than three miles; I was raised at that time at 2 o'clock, and never later than 3 o'clock.

15,257. Do you mean that someone went round the place to call the boys? –

No. The men lived more then in their own cottages in that part of the country. We got up in the morning, I being called by my father at 1, or very often at 2 o'clock. We remained then in the mines until 5 and 6 at night. It was an iron-stone mine, very low, working about 18 inches, and in some instances not quite so high.

15,258. That is, you remained 16 or 17 hours in the pit? — Yes, as a rule.

15,259. Was the work constant for a boy of that age for that time? — The work was perfectly constant.

15,260. No break? — No break. Then I removed to coal mines after that. There we had low seams also, very low seams. There we had no rails to draw upon, that is, tramways laid like rails now for our tubs, or corves, or whirlies as we call them, to run upon. We had leather belts for our shoulders. One was before and another behind, and the wheels were cutting the pavements or floor (we called it pavement) and we had to keep dragging the coal with these ropes over our shoulders, and sometimes round the middle with a chain between our legs. Then there was always another behind pushing with his head.

15,261. That work was done with children? — That work was done by boys, such as I was, from 10 or 11 down to eight, and I have known them as low as seven years old. In the mines at that time the state of ventilation was frightful.

15,262. *(Mr Mathews.)* Are you now speaking of ironstone mines or coal mines? — Of coal and ironstone mines together. The gases pervading the mines in Scotland at the time were for the most part carbonic acid gas, not carburetted hydrogen; and I remember well often having three or four lamps put together for the purpose of keeping so much light as to enable us to see by. A very great deal of our drawing, as we call it, was performed in the dark in consequence of the want of ventilation in the mines.

15,263. *(Lord Elcho.)* Did that want of ventilation at that time lead to frequent accidents? — It did not lead to frequent accidents; but it led to premature death.

15,264. Not to explosion? — No; carbonic acid gas in no case leads to explosion. There was no explosive gas in those mines I was in, or scarcely any. I may state incidentally here that in the first ironstone mine I was in there were some 20 or more boys besides myself, and I am not aware at this moment that there is one alive excepting myself.

Alexander MacDonald, Evidence given before the Royal Commission on Trades Unions, Wednesday 28 April 1868 (Parliamentary Papers, 1867-8, vol. 39, pp. 38-9

Source 5
The Wynds of Glasgow

The wynds of Glasgow comprise a fluctuating population of from fifteen to twenty thousand persons. This quarter consists of a labyrinch of lanes, out of which numberless entrances lead into small courts, each with a dunghill reeking in the centre. Revolting as was the outside of those places, I was little prepared for the filth and destitution within. In some of those lodging houses (visited at night) we found a whole lair of human beings littered along the floor — sometimes fifteen and twenty, some clothed and some naked — men, women and children huddled promiscuously together. . . .A very extensive inspection of the lowest districts of other places, both here and on the continent, never presented anything half so bad, either in intensity of pestilence, physical and moral, or in extent proportioned to the population.

Source 6
Chadwick and the Public Health Act

Probably the greatest virtue of Chadwick's *Report on the Sanitary Condition of the Labouring Population of Great Britain* was its handling of statistical evidence which conclusively established the incontrovertible link between environment and disease. . .To find that the death rate in Cheetham was 1 in 45 while that in nearby Manchester was 1 in 26, or that the rate in the Leeds suburb of Chapeltown was 1 in 57 while that in the central area, Kirkgate, was twice as high at 1 in 28, was to indicate the environmental origin of disease. To demonstrate the sociological and geographic variations in life expectancy was to establish a close correlation between insanitary housing, deficient sewerage and water supply with the incidence of disease, high death rate and low expectation of life. This was the main and crucial element in the case the report was trying to establish. The economic cost of disease with which Chadwick began was by 1842 a relatively minor factor, though easily demonstrated by reference to the numbers of widows and orphans. Chadwick was much more interested in demonstrating the social evils *consequent* upon insanitary living conditions, and he turned current social theory on its head by arguing that the low moral standards (intemperance, prostitution, delinquency, etc.) were the result of the domestic physical environment, not the other way round.

Chadwick was convinced that the environmental controls necessary to *prevent* disease would require more powerful administrative organs than existed even within the reformed corporations. He wanted in fact a centralised and uniform administrative structure similar to that which he had suggested for the Poor Law, yet his final conclusions in the report were vague and rather unsatisfactory on this point. Far more definite was his solution to the civil engineering problem of sewage disposal. He strongly advocated the water-borne disposal of sewage via glazed round pipes which is of course the modern method. . . Inevitably this would place even greater demands upon water supply, which became even more essential. Hence the search for even more efficient modes of supplying urban areas with water both for consumption and drainage was a logical consequence of the evidence accumulated in the report. Indeed Chadwick assumed that the presentation of the case required few definite conclusions, since these would gradually evolve from the debate initiated by the report, and his only other major suggestion was the appointment of district medical officers.

Perhaps the greatest of the nineteenth-century Blue Books, the Chadwick Report, had an unprecedented sale for an official publication, possibly as high as 100,000. The Poor Law Commissioners had refused in the event to sign the report, which was thus circulated under Chadwick's sole name. Public complacency was certainly shattered and the early Victorian conscience was aroused, yet Chadwick knew that his report was only the beginning of what would be a long and arduous propaganda campaign. In 1843 he wrote a report on interment, arguing for the physical separation of burial grounds from urban areas, and in 1844-5 he unofficially directed the affairs of the Health and Towns Commission which the Peel Government set up, in effect to validate the evidence and conclusion of Chadwick's *personal* report. More than this, the Commission delved more deeply into the technical and administrative details of possible legislation and so took the campaign on a stage further. It remained for the Health of Towns Association, begun in 1844 and organised mainly by Southwood Smith, to pursue the propaganda campaign for the implementation of legislation which was not to come until 1848.

From Derek Fraser, *The Evolution of the British Welfare State* (McMillan 1973) pp. 58-9. Reproduced by permission of MacMillan, London and Basingstoke.

Source 7
The condition of the working classes

Since. . .the rich have all the power, the proletarians must submit. . . .to have the law actually declare them superfluous. This has been done by the New Poor Law . . .The regulation of these workhouses, or as the people call them Poor Law Bastilles, is such as to frighten away everyone who has the slightest prospect of life without this form of public charity. . .the workhouse has been made the most repulsive residence which the refined ingenuity of a Malthusian can invent.

In the workhouse at Greenwhich, in the summer of 1843, a boy five years old was punished by being shut in the dead room, where he had to sleep on the lids of the coffins. In the workhouse at Herne the same punishment was inflicted upon a little girl for wetting the bed at night. . . .

In the workhouse at Bacton, in Suffolk, in January, 1844, an investigation revealed the fact that a feeble-minded woman was employed as nurse, and took care of the patients accordingly; while sufferers who were often restless at night, or tried to get up, were tied fast with cords passed over the covering and under the bedstead, to save the nurse the trouble of sitting up at night. . .

As in life so in death. The poor are dumped into the earth like infected cattle. The pauper burial ground at St. Brides, London, is a bare morass, in use as a cemetery since the time of Charles II, and filled with a heap of bones; every Wednesday the paupers are thrown into a ditch fourteen feet deep; a curate rattles through the Litany at the top of his speed; the ditch is loosely covered in to be reopened the next Wednesday. . . .

Can anyone wonder that the poor decline to accept public relief?. . . That they starve rather than enter these Bastilles? . . .

From F. Engels, *The Condition of the Working Classes in England* (1844) reprinted in Dawson and Wall, *Society and Industry in the 19th Century: a documentary approach. 5. The Problem of Poverty.* (O.U.P. 1969) pp. 27-8.

Source 8
Railways and Glasgow

Glasgow acted more rapidly than most other large towns to secure an adequate supply of pure water. Between 1855 and 1859 it built an aqueduct from Loch Katrine to the city. This enabled the installation of fresh water taps, water-closets and public baths.

But congestion remained and got worse when railways were built into the central areas in the 1860s and 1870s. About 10,000 people were evicted from their houses to accommodate the railways to St Enoch and Central stations. This intensified the slum problem by causing increased congestion in the areas around those which were demolished.

Congestion affected not only workmen's houses but industrial premises and the pattern of the road system. The Corporation tackled all three problems in 1866 by setting up the City of Glasgow Improvement Trust. The Trust started to rebuild the oldest part of the city. It exercised powers of compulsory purchase to demolish slums, realign streets, build corporation lodging houses, and eventually build and let workmen's houses. The Trust was a pioneer effort at integrated urban reconstruction, and one of the showpieces of a Corporation which by the end of the century prided itself on the number and variety of its enterprises in what came to be known as 'municipal socialism'. By 1900 it owned four gasworks, two electricity generating stations, art galleries, concert halls, hospitals, farms, markets and seventy-two miles of tramway lines.

Plainly, if you demolish slums and reduce population densities in the centre of the city, and industry continues to expand, especially on the outskirts of the city, workers find it more difficult to live near their work. Cheap public transport facilities become desirable.

In the 1870s and 1880s special workmen's trains started to operate on the railways, with fares as low as 2d for a journey of eight to ten miles; horse and steam trams were introduced, and the river authority started a service of little steamboats which plied up and down the Clyde between the city centre and the shipyards.

But all these were overshadowed by the Corporation's intervention in the field of urban transport. When the tramways were first built in 1872, the Corporation owned the tracks and leased them to a private company. When the lease ended in 1894 it took over operation and, after taking stock of the most recent developments in tramway equipment, electrified the lines and extended the system. The takeover meant that the profits of tramway operation went not to the company shareholders but to the citizens of Glasgow in the shape of low fares.

By the 1900s tramway competition was challenging the suburban railways and forcing them to improve services and reduce fares. Access to public transport in particular, the tram and the Clyde paddle steamer on which Glasgow people got away from the city to the Clyde coast on summer weekends, became part of the popular culture of the city.

I have been using mechanised transport in this section as an example of the benefits which were produced by the 'industrialising' of an activity, and of the way in which these benefits were allocated. In the case of the railways of Glasgow, we have seen how they were first built to cater for the mineral needs of the industries of the area, then how they were promoted to compete with existing carriers like canals and so reduce the transport costs of materials. Then local investors started to project lines, with mixed motives of developing the locality and making a profit for themselves. Finally the idea of the railway as a profitable investment pure and simple took over and London speculators put up money for Scottish railways.

From *A100, An Arts Foundation Course* (Open University) Units 29-30, pp. 132-3. *The original A100 course has now been replaced by a new foundation course (A101) which was first presented in 1978.*

COURSE COMMENTS

We would be interested to hear your reactions to this course. Send your comments to Courses Editor, NEC, 18 Brooklands Avenue, Cambridge CB2 2HN.

Name . . . .

Student Number . . . .

Address . . . .

. . . .

. . . .

Clear Thinking